William Cheetham

Christianity Reviewed

William Cheetham

Christianity Reviewed

ISBN/EAN: 9783337241773

Printed in Europe, USA, Canada, Australia, Japan

Cover: Foto ©Lupo / pixelio.de

More available books at **www.hansebooks.com**

CHRISTIANITY REVIEWED.

BY THE

REV. WILLIAM CHEETHAM.

AUTHOR OF

"LIGHTS AND SHADOWS OF CLERICAL LIFE."

"The voice of one crying in the wilderness, prepare ye the way of the Lord, make His paths straight.—*Matt. 3 chap. 3 v.*

BROCKVILLE:
THE RECORDER PRINTING COMPANY.
1896.

CONTENTS.

CHAPTER I.
The Bible from a Common Sense Standpoint.

CHAPTER II.
Handling the Word of God.

CHAPTER III.
The Inconsistencies of Professing Christians.

CHAPTER IV.
Church Methods and Work.

CHAPTER V.
Prayer.

CHAPTER VI.
The Prayer Meeting.

CHAPTER VII.
The Philosophy of Salvation.

CHAPTER VIII.
The Duty of Supporting the Gospel.

CHAPTER IX.
The Pastoral Relation.

CHAPTER X.
The Ethics of Christianity.

TO THE MEMORY OF MY ONLY SON,

WHOSE DEATH,

DEEPLY LAMENTED,

GAVE FORTH THE GERM AND QUICKENING

FROM WHICH THESE PAGES HAVE

SPRUNG,

THIS VOLUME IS AFFECTIONATELY INSCRIBED

BY

THE AUTHOR.

PREFACE.

Christianity is more a life than a creed, and as such it is reviewed in the following pages. The author is just presumptuous enough to indulge the hope that his book may do some good. That has been his object in writing it, if he understands himself. Whether there is need for it the Christian public must judge. The author, at least, thinks there is. There are many things said that need to be said, and that he has long waited for an opportunity to say.

The reader will find nothing of a sectarian nature here. The matters treated are, for the most part, common to all denominations of Christians, and they are very practical. Truth has not been sacrificed, neither has charity been neglected. It is not expected that all the views advanced will meet with universal approval. It would be a denial of average human experience to indulge such an expectation. If, however, they meet with anything like general attention, thought will likely be stimulated in some useful directions, and as that is the precursor of action, something practical may result.

The preachers have not escaped criticism, neither have they lacked a bold and fearless defence when necessary; and both, it is claimed, within the limits of truth and charity. They may pick up a hint, here and there, worth remembering; and they will find that some things have been said that will tend to their easement and better appreciation. Many things, pertaining to Christians and to Christian Churches, have been dealt with in a kindly but faithful spirit; that kindliness which is founded upon truth, and that faithfulness which springs from the love of truth.

Indeed it is fervently hoped that the following pages may be found, in some humble measure, "profitable for doctrine, for reproof, for correction, for instruction in righteousness."

CHAPTER I.

The Bible, from a Common Sense Standpoint.

AM I absolutely sure that the Bible is what it claims to be, a Divinely inspired book? I frankly admit I am not. Is its Divine origin capable of absolute demonstration? I do not think it is. Can the candid mind reach a point in its enquiries where not a shadow of doubt rests upon the validity of its claims? I think not. What then? Are we to give the Bible up, and cast it away from us? By no means. What we have to do, however, is to be more reasonable in our claims, and juster in our defence, than we have hitherto been. We are dealing with intelligent men, in a wide-awake age, who will not accept assumption for argument, nor mere dogmatism for clear and reasonable proof. We must not atttempt the impracticable, and the impossible.

We must not try to explain everything, and harmonize everything. Above all we must be honest; that is, we must not be slow to admit what is clearly our duty to admit, though the admission may seem, in some measure, to militate against the claims in which we so fervently believe, and for which we so earnestly contend. The Bible has been injured, in the past, by the unwise advocacy of its well meaning, but sadly mistaken friends. It might justly cry, deliver me from my friends; at least from some of them. The fact is undeniable that untenable and unnecessary claims have been put forth in its behalf, and too little has been conceded to the logic of facts, and the dictates of common sense.

While I do not claim, and think it unwise because untenable to claim, proof complete and absolute for the Divine origin of the Bible, I, nevertheless, give it my strong confidence, because the balance of evidence—internal and external—is overwhelmingly in its favor. And as this is the principle by which human judgment and conduct are regulated in all things—even in the commonest as well as the most momentous affairs of life, it cannot be inappropriate or exceptional to apply it to the present case. Indeed, it is the part of wisdom so to apply it, and so to rest upon it. Objection has been made against the Bible, on the ground that while it professes to be a revelation, there are some things in it not only hard, but impossible of human comprehension and understanding. The fact, as stated, must be admitted, and without quibbling or evasion. There are things hard to be understood. There are some things which transcend the faculties of the human mind. What then is the force of the objection? Does it really, and in any measure, invalidate the claims of the Book? Not at all. There are several considerations worthy of being noted in this connection.

The first is that the Book claims to be of Divine origin —that is, the product of an infinite mind—and therefore it need not be at all surprising if some things, perfectly consistent and harmonious in themselves, appear impossible of satisfactory solution to the human mind, which, at its highest and best, can never be anything but finite; that is, necessarily limited in its scope and range.

The second consideration is, that it is probably one of the prime intentions of the Book not only to affirm, which it frequently does, the necessary limitations of human knowledge, but to give full and ample illustrations of the same, as an incentive to a becoming humility in the midst of our increasing knowledge.

The third consideration is that, what we know not now we may know hereafter. By this is meant not only the possibility of development in knowledge in the future state—which is clearly and plainly predicted and promised—but also the possibility of such increased acquisitions in what remains to us of the present life ; or if not to us to succeeding generations of men, if such acquisitions are deemed by the All-Wise necessary and useful. The Bible is adapted not only to all nations but to all times, and it may be a Divine intention that its truths shall be educed and understood according to the ever expanding requirements of the race.

Again, it is not unusual for the unfriendly critic to adduce certain passages of Scripture which by comparison seem contradictory, and he instantly assumes and affirms that they are so, when, in fact, rightly considered and interpreted, they are not. Viewed verbally, and intellectually they may be opposed, and in some cases radically so, but looked at spiritually, that is, by the aid of what the Scriptures call spiritual discernment, and in the light of a sanctified Christian experience, there is at once seen a harmony which is both beautiful and profound. Spiritual things in order to be understood must be spiritually discerned. That is the dictum of the Book itself, and we must be honest enough to take it on its own ground. "The natural man receiveth not the things of the Spirit of God, for they are foolishness unto him, neither can he know them, because they are spiritually discerned." 1st Cor. 2 ch. 14 v. Thus there is a spiritual faculty—a new-birth faculty, it might be called —not inherent in man naturally nor intellectually, but given to the earnest seeker under certain specified conditions; a faculty essentially distinct from the intellectual, and yet necessarily allied with it in its exercise, and by the aid of which the harmony and beauty of spiritual truth may be clearly perceived.

Numerous illustrations of this might be given. Let one suffice. Take those three oft-repeated passages on burden-bearing, "For every man shall bear his own burden," Gal. 6 ch., 5 v.; "Bear ye one another's burdens and so fulfil the law of Christ," Gal. 6 ch , 2 v.; "Cast thy burden upon the Lord, and he shall sustain thee," Psalm 55 ch., 22 v. Now, viewed from a verbal and merely intellectual standpoint, these passages may be safely and frankly admitted to be self-contradictory. They all refer to the same thing, burden-bearing; but something essentially different, as far as action is concerned, is predicted in each case. In the first you have to bear your own burden. In the second you share it with another. In the third you cast it upon God. Are they, in their proper relation and meaning, antagonistic? Not at all. A blessed harmony, in the seemingly inharmonious, is clearly seen by the soul that is taught by the Spirit of God, and by a sanctified Christian experience. Responsibility, as a central thought, inheres in each passage. In the first we have personal responsibility; in the second mutual responsibility; in the third Divine responsibility. Where personal responsibility ends mutual responsibility begins, and where mutual responsibility ends Divine responsibility begins. Instead of being mutually destructive they are mutually consistent and helpful. There is a logical sequence leading to a complete harmony of statement, of sentiment, and of thought.

Passing from this let me here observe that there are some things, in regard to the Bible, that it is neither wise, necessary, nor useful to contend for. I emphatically, and in the plainest possible way, state, that my deep conviction is, that it is not wise, it is not necessary, it is not useful to contend that the Bible, as we have it, is a perfect book, containing an absolutely adequate expression of the depth and splendor of the Divine thought. It may be, and probably is, sufficient for our safe guidance, but that falls short of the perfect and the absolute. Indeed, from the very nature of the case, it must be more or less inadequate when we take into account the imperfect media through which it has come to us. How can a Divine thought be adequately expressed in human language? How can the finite hold the infinite? As soon, and sooner in fact, might you expect to engulf Jupiter in this little globe of ours.

Indeed this inadequacy—and inevitable inadequacy—is recognized by the record itself. Christ evidently felt the insufficiency of human language to convey the fulness of the Divine thought that was in Him when He said to Nicodemus : "For God so loved the world, that he gave his only begotten son, that whosoever believeth in him should not perish, but have everlasting life." John 3 ch. 16 v. Clearly, how much God loved the world words could not express, and the use of the word so recognises the impotency. There was a great thought laboring for expression, and it had to go forth without full expression, and was left in an indefinite state. Neither can it be measured by our conception, because that is finite, as we are, and the love is infinite, as God is.

Then the apostle Paul seemed to labor under the same difficulty in that matchless utterance of his about affliction : "For our light affliction, which is but for a moment, worketh for us a far more exceeding and eternal weight of glory." 2 Cor. 4 ch. 17 v. He piles one epithet upon another in a vain endeavor to reach the splendor and immensity of the thought, and then takes refuge in that momentous word *eternal*—so grand, and yet so indefinite, and incomprehensible to finite minds to express the magnitude of the heavenly reward which is in store for the afflicted believer.

I will further state here that, it is neither wise, necessary, nor useful to contend for the absolute verbal accuracy of the Bible. Why? Because as a matter of fact, it is not only not probable, but, under the circumstances, it does not seem possible: at least, the possibility is so contingent and so remote as to make it practically worthless. It can be readily seen that when this concession is made—as it may be without diminishing in any appreciable degree the just weight and authority of the record—you cut the ground from beneath the feet of a thousand objectors. Does a verbal inaccuracy, or a number of verbal inaccuracies, invalidate any book, or make it unreadable, or not understandable. As a matter of fact they do not. Indeed, we expect to find them, and we should be rather surprised than otherwise if we did not; for we know that in some measure they are inevitable in any book, the production of which is dependant, in whole or in part, upon the imperfect intelligence and mechanical activities of man. God is infallible, necessarily so, but man is not; and so long as He works in conjunction with the human, in the production of any given result, a certain amount of necessary imperfection must ensue.

Please to observe, however, that I am not, at present, admitting that there are verbal inaccuracies in the Bible: neither am I contending that there are not. The force of the argument is not dependant upon any admission one way or the other. I admit, and I think any reasonable man will admit, when I have done, that the Bible is of God; that it is a divine book; that it is not simply a human production; that men were inspired by the Holy Ghost to write it, and that they were guarded against error in so doing. But I frankly confess I am not prepared to admit that the men who copied the sacred writings, through all the intervening centuries, were equally, or even partially, inspired, and guarded against, error, in what was purely a mechanical operation. And I am not prepared to admit that the men, good as they were, who, from time to time, translated or revised the Book were inspired, and guarded against error. And if these men were not inspired in transcribing, translating, and revising, verbal inaccuracy to a certain extent—that is, to the extent of the necessary and well known imperfections of man—is not only possible, but exceedingly probable. It is what we might reasonably expect; and to think otherwise, or affirm otherwise is to flatly deny the clearest dictates of reason and common sense.

Having cleared the way thus far, by answering certain objections, and by frankly admitting what the probable facts and the necessity of the case seem to call for, we are entitled to proceed with the main enquiry, namely: Is the Bible what it professes to be, the word of God? Is it of Divine origin? And if so is the evidence clearly discernible by the candid mind, and is it of such a nature that it ought to carry conviction with it? I think it is.

I. The first consideration to be submitted is, that there is a strong presumption, from the nature and constitution of things, in favor of a revelation, and such a revelation as the Bible claims to be, and is. This argument may be thus briefly stated.

Assuming the existence of God—and we may be allowed to assume it for the present purpose—and that we are His creatures, His children if you like that term better, the work of His hands, and the objects of His solicitude and care, dependent upon Him physically, mentally and morally, it is reasonable to suppose that He would not leave us without a revelation of His will to guide us. Judging by the analogy of nature and human experience the thing is at least probable. There are many things pertaining to us personally and our relation to Him, necessary for us to know, and concerning which He alone could instruct us. We think it necessary, and it is necessary, not only to care for and support our children, but also to instruct and guide them. In short, to let them know, from time to time, what our will is concerning them, and this is necessary for their well-being. Surely God, the Infinite Father, is not likely to do less than we; not likely to be less mindful than we are; not likely, in fact, to omit such a revelation of His character, and such an expression of His will as are necessary for our enlightenment and safe guidance. So that a revelation, and such a revelation as the Bible contains is clearly probable, and constitutes a strong presumption in its favor.

II. Not only is a Divine revelation probable, but it is necessary. There are many things which nature, and reason, and science may explain, with more or less of completeness and satisfaction, but there are other things, of great and lasting importance to us, upon which they are as silent as the grave.

There is not even an answering echo to our deep and anxious enquiries, Whence am I? What am I? And whither am I going? The origin, the nature, and the destiny of man are insoluble problems apart from the Bible. As to the first, the origin of man, science knows nothing and can say nothing. As to the second, the nature of man, it may offer some descriptions or explanations of a materialistic kind, that is in regard to what is apparent to the senses, but the deeper and real nature, with its insatiable longings and far reaching aspirations, it cannot touch. As to the third, the destiny of man, it is as impotent as it is in regard to the first—that is, it knows nothing, and can say nothing. And yet we want these questions answered. It seems necessary to our comfort and well-being that they should be answered. They will not back down, and out. They will force themselves to the front. They voice themselves in our inmost consciousness. They cry aloud, and spare not. Whence? What? Whither? Reason is silent. Nature is silent. Science, the interpretation, and classification of nature, is silent. The Bible alone is vocal, and is our only reliance and interpreter. It tells me I am of God, and from God; that I am made of the visible and the invisible, body and soul; and that I am tending in the direction of fixity and eternity; an eternity unspeakable in its nature and possibilities.

Other questions arise in the thoughtful and earnest mind, equally profound and important, and equally insoluble apart from the Bible, such as: Why am I perpetually dissatisfied with all things earthly? Why am I constantly drawn in the direction of natural, mental and moral disintegration? Whence this constant tendency to the evil in preference to the good? Why must I suffer so much in this world, and especially why must I suffer so much through the wrong-doing of others? I know I must die, because it is the universal experience, but why must I die? What is the reason of it? Why cannot the present state of being, and present relationship, be continued endlessly? Why must I give up a certainty for what, if it be not an uncertainty, is, at least, an uncertain quantity? Why do I heave my aching heart, and stretch out my feeble hands, and articulate with my faltering tongue, and peer with my glistening eyes into the dark future after the vanished form?

Why all this? These and other questions come unbidden, unsought. They well up in the mind involuntarily, and bid us seek, and seek earnestly, the possible answer. We have a right to ask, and we have a right to seek. It is not meant we should be ignorant where knowledge, by lawful means, is attainable. Close your Bibles, and you must remain in the dark. You may think, and think until nature is exhausted, and you will think in vain. These problems are too deep for a merely intellectual solution. They call for a Divine one, and that, in the nature of the case, must be a revelation, by some connecting agency, from on high. There is something terribly wrong in this world. Things are out of joint. There should be harmony, and peace, and contentment, and light, and perpetuation of life; but instead, the sad experience of all men in all ages testifies, we have confusion, strife, dissatisfaction, darkness, suffering, separation, death. Why? The Bible furnishes the answer. It speaks of something it calls sin, and it defines sin as the transgression of the law, the law of God. That explains everything. That furnishes the key to these manifold difficulties and perplexities. That shows us why we are as we are. That is the prime root and cause of all that afflicts humanity. Take sin out of the world, and the change would be marvellous and complete.

III. Then look at the *purity* of the Bible. It is so pure in its tone, so elevated in its morality, so exceptional and original in its teaching, so impartial in its history of men and nations—even the most exalted and the most favored—so consistent in its denunciation of all impurity and wrong doing, and so constant in its upholding of what is pure and right, that it is incredible to suppose that it had simply a human origin. Where did the ten Commandments – the Moral Law—come from? How did they originate? What mind gave birth to that marvellously perfect, all-embracing, far-reaching, and enduring code. It was put forth in what was really, as compared with the present, a dark and barbarous age. Certainly it was not an age distinguished for moral excellence as we understand morality. Certainly the most favored nation in the world at that time—God's chosen people—had not within it a man of intellect so gigantic, and moral proportions so colossal, as to produce such a code. It was not likely to emanate from any human source in such an age as that, nor for the matter of that in any age. The only way to arrive at a reasonable and satisfactory solution is by admitting the correctness of the record, that it came from God, and in the time and manner there stated. Then, turning from the old to the new Testament, look at the teaching of Jesus Christ. Take that peerless utterance, which has been the wonder of the intellectual and moral world for over eighteen hundred years, the Sermon on the Mount. How it shines still, after the lapse of centuries, in its pure crystalline brightness and unfading glory. It is so pure—so incisively pure, if such an expression may be used, that it strikes deep down into the inmost recesses of the human heart, and tracks the motive as well as the act, the intention as well as the execution of the intention. A man must not only not do evil, he must not think evil, for God will call him to account for the one as well as the other. Now as far as human law is concerned—even in this advanced age, and amongst nations of the highest probity, culture, and moral advancement—we never entertain the thought of calling a man to account for thinking evil, much less punishing him; and what is more, we are utterly incompetent to do it. He may think as much evil as he likes, and as long as he likes; he is safe from punishment so long as his thoughts, however vile, do not mature into words and acts that may operate to the disadvantage and injury of others. Surely, this is a Divine principle which lays hold of the motive, and makes a man responsible for evil intention, or unlawful desire that stops short of the act. It certainly is not of the human, nor is it within the competence of the human.

IV. Then let us also consider that the *unity* of truth in the Bible is as remarkable as its purity, and points to the same origin. Now whatever adverse criticism may be offered in regard to any isolated portion of Scripture, or indeed, if you like, in regard to the whole, one thing, in all fairness should be conceded, and that is that there is a oneness about it, and that all the books of the Old and New Testament are substantially one book.

One grand increasing purpose runs through the whole, from Genesis to Revelation, the education, uplifting and recovery of a lost race. No sooner is the sad fact stated of the fall of the first pair—as it is in one of the earliest chapters—than the Deliverer is announced and promised; and the great and beneficent enterprise is] steadily in view unto the last chaper, and almost the last verse of the last book that the volume contains.

Let it also be borne in mind that while the Bible is substantially one book, it is made up of a number of books by different writers, who wrote at different times, extending over a period of fifteen hundred or two thousand years; and that these writers were as varied in their personality, education, disposition, surroundings, experience, mental calibre, and even prejudices, as men generally are ; and yet we have a substantial and marvellous unity of truth, that cannot reasonably be accounted for on the ground of either collusion, design, or chance. The only way to account for it, without doing violence to common sense, is to frankly admit what the record claims, that " Holy men of God spake as they were moved by the Holy Ghost."

One prevailing and powerful personality dominates the whole Book, securing unity amid much that is diverse, and that personality is clearly not human but divine.

V. We have also much valuable concurrent testimony, in regard to the more ancient facts of the Bible, inscribed upon clay tablets dug out of the ruins of Nineveh, which now are, and have been for many years, treasured in the British Museum. These records, which are said to be a part of the library of the grandson of Sennacherib of Bible fame, contain accounts, more or less full, of the Creation, the Fall, the Deluge, the building of the Tower of Babel, and the Confusion of Tongues. The account of the Creation, and the Fall is said to be much longer and fuller than the record in Genesis; also some important details are added about the origin of evil, the fall of the angels, and the wickedness of the serpent. The condition of things before the creation is described as chaos, answering to the Biblical account that "the earth was without form and void, and darkness was upon the face of the deep." Creation is represented as being the work of a plurality of gods, answering to the Elohim of Genesis, which is well known to be plural, and thus giving the first intimation of the doctrine of the Trinity. Successive stages marked the creation of the world, answering to the Bible days, or the indefinite periods of time which science calls for. At each stage in the porcess the work is pronounced good. Then man "is made upright, and free from evil, and endowed with the noble faculty of speech." God instructs him in his duty, but he yields to temptation and falls; then the curse is pronounced, and its effects fall upon him and his posterity, producing all the attendant evils which have ever since afflicted humanity. Mention is also made of the fall, through ambition, of a Celestial Being of great intelligence and power, of a war in heaven, and of the defeat and final overthrow of the conspiring and rebellious powers; answering to the Scripture references to Satan, "and the Angels which kept not their first estate."

One of the most interesting records is that about the Deluge, which is, in all the main and important points, the same as the Mosaic account. Here it is in brief, according to the translation of Mr. George Smith of the British Museum: "A great flood was sent upon the earth to punish men for their wickedness. One man, Sisit, receives a Divine warning, and a command to build a huge ship, and to take into it a chosen few only of mankind, together with some of all other living things. The flood came, then subsided; the ship grounded upon a mountain; birds were sent out and returned twice, but the third time returned no more. Then Sisit went forth, built an altar, and made a sacrifice."

These are important confirmatory evidences of the integrity and accuracy of the sacred record, and they are all the time increasing. New and even more important discoveries are being made. The hoary past has become vocal. The earth has lifted up its voice. The very stones are crying out, and claiming to be heard. Even the long lost sepulchres of the illustrious dead have opened, and given their testimony. The bodies of some of the ancient kings—the Pharaohs of Egypt—have been found and identified beyond any doubt; and so perfect was the art preservative among the Egyptians that after three thousand years or more they are in a perfect state of preservation. You may travel to Egypt, and enter the museum at Bulak, and there see the very form and features of Seti I. the father of that "Pharoah's daughter" who rescued the infant Moses from the Nile, and the man who issued that infamous edict for the slaying of all the male children of an enslaved and oppressed people. And along with it you can see that of his son Rameses II.—called Rameses the Great—and so perfectly has the decay of nature been arrested, by the marvellous art of the Egyptians, that after the lapse of thirty-two centuries, while there is a difference in the two faces—the father's being more refined than that of the son—there is nevertheless an astonishing and unmistakable likeness.

Rameses II. was said to be a great man—great in battle and conquest, great in building palaces and temples which even in their ruin and decay are the wonder and astonishment of the world but he was emphatically a hard man, brutal we might say. He, even more than his father, was an oppressor, and his fearful exactions and unrelentless cruelty made the enslaved race groan by reason of their bondage, and cry mightily unto God for deliverance.

Let me explain here, parenthetically, to guard against a possible misapprehension, that the body of the Pharaoh of the plagues, the hardened heart, and the exodus—Menephtah, son of Rameses II.—has not been found. Probably it never will be. He may have found a nameless grave, with the pursuing host, in the Red Sea. At least, the non-discovery, up to date, is significant and suggestive.

There they are, those two, Seti and Rameses, father and son, side by side in that museum at Bulak. Over three thousand years have gone by since they lived, and moved, and had a being. Conjointly and singly they ruled a mighty empire for near upon a century, if not quite. They lived sumptuously, ruled despotically, built palaces and temples of surpassing magnitude and grandeur, fought battles, made extensive conquests, and under them the empire attained its zenith of renown and glory. They were worshipped as gods, and yet they had to pay the debt of nature, and die as other mortals die.

They were embalmed with an exquisite art, and decked with gold, and silver, and all manner of precious stones, and then carefully and secretly put away in the royal sepulchre, in the valley of the Tombs of the Kings, under the Theban hills. After a period of silence and forgetfulness, equal to a full half of the entire history of the human race, a chance discovery brings them forth again to the light of day. In the presence of competent witnesses the wrappings were carefully removed, the inscriptions and symbols noted, and the identification completed, and established beyond reasonable doubt. Those uncovered faces, full of life-like expression even yet, and gazed at by the passing tourist, hush the soul in awe, and speak volumes to the reverent mind. They have a language all their own, and an eloquence which death and the reverberating centuries can alone inspire, and say to us in deeply solemn and admonitory tones, in the words of Holy Writ: "Let not the wise man glory in his wisdom, neither let the mighty man glory in his might; let not the rich man glory in his riches, but let him that glorieth glory in this, that he understandeth and knoweth me, that I am the Lord which exercise loving-kindness, judgment and righteousness in the earth." Jer. 9 c. 23-24 v.

And to the unbeliever—who has tried to persuade

himself and others that these ancient facts of Biblical history are simply pleasant myths and legends fit only for the entertainment of children—they utter a stern rebuke, and call for a reasonable exercise of faith in the unity of the word of God.

VI. Consciousness, or the answer of the human soul to the Divine word, is perhaps the most important, and the most convincing evidential consideration in regard to this subject. At least, after a good deal of thought, I am disposed to assign it that pre-eminent position. What do I mean by the answer of the human soul to the Divine word? I mean this, that the Bible strikes me as being remarkably unlike all other books. So much higher, purer, better in every respect as to, at least, suggest that its origin cannot be human. It is, in fact, unique. Even in a literary point of view it is admitted by the best authorities to be unrivalled. Then, there are references in it to certain things which it is almost incredible to suppose were within the scope of human knowledge at the time they were made. Isaiah speaks of God as "He that sitteth upon the circle of the earth," 40 ch., 22 v. Every school boy knows, or should know, that the knowledge of the rotundity of the earth is a comparatively modern acquisition. At least, we have no evidence that it was understood in the times of Isaiah. The strong probability is that it was not. Then how did the idea get into the prophet's mind, except from a source other than human, in fact, Divine. Then again Job says, chap. 26, 7 v.: "He stretcheth out the north over the empty place, and hangeth the earth upon nothing." If that is not a clear recognition and statement of the law of gravitation I shall have to give up trying to understand what language means. We know that gravitation is a modern discovery, and perhaps the greatest ever was made, or ever will be. And yet there we have it in that ancient record. How did it get there? Where did it come from? Was it human or Divine? It is not necessary, for the force of the argument, to suppose that the Old Patriarch understood the nature of the law, of which his statement is an illustration, or its boundless extent and application. Probably he did not, but it is there neverthless, and common sense must recognize it, and admit that it came from a higher source than he. In other words, it was a little bit of light shot straight from heaven, through the mouth of this ancient man, giving the first intimation of that law which enfolds the universe in its grasp, and which the wisdom and researches of the wisest and the best, for centuries upon centuries, failed to discover.

Then take a reference of a somewhat different nature, but illustrating the same point, Isaiah's prediction regarding the Coming Deliverer, 9 ch., 6 v.: "For unto us a child is born, unto us a son is given: and the government shall be upon his shoulders; and his name shall be called Wonderful, Counsellor, The Mighty God, The Everlasting Father, The Prince of Peace." The literary excellence and moral grandeur of that forecast of the future is simply unapproachable. What a reach of pure and elevated thought! What a combination of epithets! What a climax! I am not unmindful of the many samples of rare eloquence which we have, and which the memory of a moderately informed man may recall. Of Dante's force and fire, and intensely realistic descriptions. Of Shakespeare's profundity, wide knowledge, marvellous reach of thought, and felicity of expression. Of the melting pathos of Milton's Eve's lament on leaving Paradise. Of the profound religious tone and impressive diction of Burns' Cottar's Saturday night. Of Burke's matchless eloquence in his peroration on the impeachment of Warren Hastings. Of Macaulay's polished periods and rhetorical climaxes in his description of the Puritans in the essay on Milton. All these and more may easily be recalled, but they "pale their ineffectual fire," and sink into comparative nothingness before the simple majesty of the Old Seer's prophetic utterance.

And then look at what follows in the 7th verse: "Of the increase of his government and peace there shall be no end." Whoever heard of a government without an end before? How came such a thought to the surface at all? Is there anything in the wide range of human experience to suggest it? Is there aught in ancient or modern history to give it birth? Nothing! Absolutely nothing! It is notoriously universal that human governments have an end, and sometimes a very speedy one. There has been no exception to the rule thus far, and it is not likely there ever will be.

I repeat, where did that thought come from? There is only one reasonable and common sense answer. It came from above. It is a Divine conception, relating to a Divine person, and a Divine government; for perpetuity cannot be predicted or affirmed of that which is human.

We have been dealing with Old Testament references; take one now from the New as an example of what might be produced from that source. Paul in his defence before Agrippa—Acts 26 ch. 13 v.—says. "At midnight, O king, I saw in the way a light from heaven, above the brightness of the sun, shining round about me and them which journeyed with me." That, both as to the phenomenon itself and the expression of it, is very unique. Who, except Paul, under these extraordinary circumstances, ever had cognizance of a light above the brightness of the sun. And we may fairly assume that he had no such experience before, and therefore nothing to suggest either the thought or the expression. The sun is by far the brightest object within the sphere of human vision, and therefore no man of himself, and under ordinary circumstances, would be likely to conceive and formulate such an expression.

The conclusion is plain and irresistible, namely, that here we have a remarkable fact stated, and stated in such a manner, that it strikes us as something other than human, and far above and beyond the human.

These instances might be multiplied, but I forbear, and perhaps wisely. I have not made this aspect of the subject a matter of special or extended investigation for the present writing, but have simply given such illustrations as are immediately within my present recollection. Others there are, and many, and perhaps more forcible than these I have given. I scarcely ever read the Bible without coming across some thought, or fact, or peculiarity of expression that strikes me with astonishment, and appeals to my consciousness in favor of its claim to be the very word of God, and the revelation of his will to man.

The Bible is both the foundation and the text book of Christianity. I have made some attempt to pass its claims under review, not from a critical, but from a common sense standpoint.

It is eminently a common sense Book, and is most fairly treated, and best served by a common sense defence. Get rid of the notion, once for all, and as quickly as possible, that it is necessary to understand, and explain, and harmonize everything in order to believe in it as an inspired record. Such a consummation is neither practical, nor necessary. If the weight of evidence inclines in its favor, you are bound as a reasonable man to accept it; and if you accept it, you are bound as an honest man to live by it.

CHAPTER II.

Handling the Word of God.

THERE can be no doubt about the importance of the Word of God, and the responsibility of handling it. There are many directions and admonitions given. The Apostle Paul gives one, which, combining the negative and the positive, is at the same time a valuable piece of autobiography. "Therefore seeing we have this ministry, as we have received mercy, we faint not; but have renounced the hidden things of dishonesty, not walking in craftiness, nor handling the word of God deceitfully; but by manifestation of the truth commending ourselves to every man's conscience in the sight of God;" 2 Cor., 4 ch., 1, 2 vs. The whole scope and meaning of this statement seems to be, that as far as the apostle was concerned, in his ministry, he gave the Word of God a strictly honest treatment. He put away dishonesty, craftiness, and deceit, and depended upon a straightforward presentation of the truth. Whatever others might do, he would not resort to any tricks. Model man, and model minister! Where are your successors today? Are they few or many? Paul answereth not, and until some one does, of equal experience and authority, the question may safely be left open.

Then, it is possible for a man to be dishonest, and crafty, and deceitful in handling the Word of God? Well, that is plainly implied in what the apostle says; and it is not at all improbable that his mind, at that time, was painfully dwelling upon some signal examples of this strange perversity, which had come under his own observation. Perversity did I say? It is altogether too mild a word. Strike that out and write depravity, and in large letters too, for he who is not honest in such a business is certainly depraved.

Let it be observed here, that a man handles the Word of God deceitfully when he attempts to handle it at all — that is, with a view to the edification of others— without the proper and necessary qualifications for such an important work. Manifestly he is conveying a false impression, for the expectation, and the just expectation, is that he is capable of doing that for which upon trial he is found unfit. He commences by deceiving himself, and ends by deluding others. Truly was it said by One who spake much truth, "The children of this world are, in their generation, wiser than the children of light." In the world, and in all secular occupations and callings, a man is invariably expected to be fitted by special training and experience for his work. He doesn't rely upon luck, or chance, or inspiration, for the right discharge of important functions and duties. He must be taught, and he must learn before he can perform aright and successfully, and especially before he can become an efficient instructor of others.

How is it that common sense and human experience are ignored, in regard to the most exalted work that man can engage in, namely, "handling the Word of God." In these days there is a growing impression among many, I fear a great many, that every man who is converted, or professes to be converted, is at once able, and that it his duty, to handle the Word of God to the edification of others. Any man may speak as far as he knows, that is, as far as he is really educated and qualified; but the truth is that converted novices are liable to go beyond their actual acquirements, and assume that they are as capable, as the most educated and experienced, to do that for which their present acquirements and experience do not fit them. They will sometimes go farther than this, and assume that they have a special endowment of wisdom and enlightenment, by which they are enabled to instruct the most instructed in the deep things of God; while, at every step, they are palpably manifesting their incompetence, and injuring the cause of truth which they sincerely wish to serve.

Do I wish to discourage these novices in the faith? Yes, to the extent of inducing them to cultivate a diffidence which fits their immaturity, and is really charming, and a modesty which is very becoming. No, if you mean would I frown down all their attempts at increase in knowledge, and usefulness. They must begin somewhere, and that is at the bottom of the ladder of Divine knowledge, and ascend gradually. They must learn before they begin to teach, and it is advisable always to keep within the limits of personal experience, and well-ascertained truth.

Nor is this unwisdom confined to young believers. I have seen and heard old believers, old in faith and in years, get up in a meeting, and read a chapter containing the profoundest truths, and without previous thought, or even pretence of preparation, launch out into a disconnected incoherent explanation, to the disgust of the hearers and the injury of the truth.

When will men, even good men, learn that the most serious, and the most responsible business any man can undertake is "handling the Word of God." A very great man once said, "Who is sufficient for these things?"

I fear that that widespread and useful organization, for which every lover of his fellow men must cherish a sincere respect, the Salvation Army, will not pass entirely without some adverse criticism in this connection. That the organization has met a real need, and accomplished a great deal of practical good, cannot be doubted. That it cannot be wrong for people to cry Hallelujah, and sing spiritual songs, and pray, and exhort one another to cleave to the Lord is equally beyond doubt ; but when it comes to "handling the Word of God," one has to confess that it is done, for the most part, in a crude and unsatisfactory fashion. This is no doubt mainly because the importance, the tremendous importance, of the matter is not fully realized. It is true that the ordinary Salvationist does not travel very far, or attempt much, in the way of Biblical exegesis. His remarks are generally short, and if they were as correct and pointed, in disclosing the mind of the spirit, as they are brief, they would be truly admirable and effectual. But, unfortunately, this is not the case. There is too often a pointless, endless iteration of the same things, whatever the portion of Scripture under review may be. The two words upon which the Salvationist rings all his changes are salvation and damnation, and so long as he keeps to them he is liable to be tolerably consistent in his statements; but when he travels into the region of expounding, the result is generally disappointing, and in some cases inimitably grotesque.

What about the Bible in our public schools? Is it treating the Book rightly, that is honestly, to admit it or to exclude it? Probably the majority will contend that the honest and rightful treatment is in the admission. Is the majority right? With becoming humility, and with becoming firmness I beg to confront that majority and say no, you are wrong. Unless a better argument can be adduced than any I have yet heard, for the retention of the Bible in our public schools, it is at least inexpedient to keep up a perpetual strife, and prevent a possible solution of what promises to be an endless difficulty in our educational system. Let common sense rule, and a conclusion will be reached alike just to all, to Catholic and Protestant, to believer and unbeliever, and to the Book itself. It is doubtful if the average teacher is capable, certainly not specially capable, of dealing with "the oracles of God:" and yet you require special capability in every other department of duty. For I hold that a man in order to read the Bible, with any profit to others, must have a good understanding of its deep and widely extended meaning, and must be imbued, in some measure, with devout feeling. And is it not a fact that devoutness and special knowledge of the Bible are not insisted upon as part of the necessary qualifications for teaching in a public school. And then there is another consideration, that so long as our teachers are of all shades of religious belief or disbelief—and from the necessity of the case they must ever be so—and so long as no special qualifications are required in that direction, the wisdom of making the public reading of the Bible a part of their duties may be seriously questioned.

We have arrived at such an advanced state of civilization now, that children are compelled to go to school to be educated; but no man who knows anything of the Divine nature or the Divine law will seriously contend that anyone, young or old, should be, to any extent, compelled to read the Bible; or be placed in any position where disadvantage might accrue from a seeming or real indifference. No, compulsion, even in a mild form, has no place there, nor is it in accordance with the mind of its author, whose judgment is perfect, whose will is absolute, and whose decision in any case is without appeal. The place for the Bible, or to read or teach the Bible, is in the home, the Sabbath School, and the Church, but not in the public school, where the purely secular and educational, as distinguished from the religious, is being pursued; and where a certain amount of compulsion may be lawfully exercised, that is plainly not allowable in regard to the reading of the Word of God.

I am quite aware that some wonderfully pious and orthodox people may possibly lift up their hands in holy horror, and cry heretic! unbeliever! I care not for your maledictions. I value truth above aught else, and I will not part with it to please you, or to secure your devout patronage and good opinion. And I know, too, that, as Lucretius says, "No pleasure is comparable to the standing upon the vantage ground of truth."

But what about the pulpit, that most widely extended agency for "Handling the Word of God?" Are all its occupants always honest, always truthful, never crafty nor deceitful? "Tell it not in Gath, publish it not in the streets of Askelon," I fear not. Does the man who occupies "The sacred desk" always exhibit evident qualifications and fitness for so important a function? Again I say, but in a whisper, I fear not. We are touching tender ground here, gentle reader, and we must walk softly and cautiously. When we begin commenting upon preachers you must know that we are dealing with a class of men who are proverbially sensitive, at least a little more so than some other men. I don't know what makes them so, except that, perhaps, they have not knocked about the world as much as you and I have; and they are just a little liable to stand on personal and professional dignity, which is about the worst thing a man can do if he has any real regard for his own comfort, or the comfort of the people about him. They are not all alike, of course not. ' You could scarcely expect them to be so. They vary as indefinitely and as widely as other people ; but they have many things in common, and of the things they have in common, those most prominent—that is, those most clearly recognized by others if not by themselves—are sensitiveness, professional dignity, and fallibility.

Am I going to apply the lash to the clergy? Not at all. Am I going to pronounce a fulsome eulogy? Not that either. I don't propose to do either the one or the other. As a class they are amenable to criticism the same as other people, and they generally get a good share of it. As a class they have distinguished excellencies, and, honesty will add, some weaknesses.

They have produced some of the keenest intellects and most consecrated lives that have ever illuminated the darkness of this dark world ; and they have produced some of an entirely opposite complexion ; and they have produced a very large number that might fairly be assigned a middle position between these two extremes

men of average ability, goodness, and consecration. I have met ministers of all denominations, Catholic and Protestant, whom any man must love for their sterling integrity, honesty, and truth ; and I have met others to whom my better nature and my kindliest feelings did not respond. They are human, and strange to say people are liable to lose sight of that most obvious fact and expect altogether too much from them. At present I am simply assuming the part of a critic, a kindly one I hope, with a view of pointing out some things that may be amended in regard to. that most-important function of "Handling the Word of God."

Are sufficient care and judgment exercised in the selection and education of young men for the occupancy of this important office, and the performance of these important duties? I fear not. Is the fundamental requirement, namely, the God-given faculty, sufficiently recognized and understood? Again I say, I fear not. Indeed, it may be doubted whether in a great many cases it is recognized or understood at all. This, if true, is a lamentable state of things, and it leads, and must lead, to a widespread state of inefficiency and barrenness.

Do we practically, as well as theoretically, recognize that preachers, like poets, are born not made? We should, and having found the born preacher it is our plain duty to accord him every possible chance of mental improvement and equipment, and every possible opportunity of acquiring a widely extended knowledge, of a special kind, to fit him for his life-work. At the same time we must get rid of the notion, once for all and as quickly as possible, that any young man of respectable appearance and connections, of average mental capacity, and of Christian conviction, can be educated into a preacher. It is not so. Education will educe, that is, it will draw out and develop the God-given faculty, but it cannot create it, nor confer it. A young man may be taught to make and recite a sermon correctly, and with a certain amount of efficiency perhaps, but he cannot be taught to preach one; that is God's work, resulting from an inborn faculty, and a Divine endowment and call. It is not difficult to distinguish between the reciter of sermons and the born preacher. The former reminds you of a school boy getting off his lesson, while the latter strikes you as a dominant force, and a "Master of Assemblies."

Has it ever occurred to the reader that among the thousands of good, excellent, devoted, pious, learned men who occupy our pulpits to-day, really original thinkers and preachers are, to put it charitably and mildly, in a most distinguished minority. Is it not so, and why is it so? The cause is neither obscure, nor far to seek. The fault is mainly in the beginning. No man, however well qualified otherwise, is fit to have the charge of young men who have the ministry in view, who is not himself an independent and vigorous thinker; and who is not prepared to insist upon common honesty in regard to the mental treasures of others, and the exercise of honest independent thought. They should be taught that it is their duty not to retail other men's thoughts, but to be themselves creators of thought, as they can most certainly be if they are true to themselves and the gift which is in them. Each one should be a voice, not an echo. Who would be an echo, when it is quite within his power to be a voice. And they should be further informed, kindly but firmly, that as they begin they will be likely to continue: and that if they do begin using crutches they need not be surprised if they discover, some day, that they have lost the use of their legs, and are cripples for life, and objects of pity, if not of contempt.

This touches the root of a good deal of manifest pulpit inefficiency to day. There is altogether too much dependence upon "Pulpit Aids," "Sketches of Sermons," "Homiletic Reviews," and "Sermons by distinguished Preachers"; and too little dependence upon painstaking, independent thought, and patient, personal investigation of the Word of God. A great statesman once said that a man who does not speak his own thoughts cannot be interesting, and he might have added cannot be effective.

> "This above all—to thine own self be true;
> And it must follow, as the night the day,
> Thou canst not then be false to any man."

One source of weakness in the pulpit, which is to be sincerely deplored, and which is clearly apparent to the intelligent observer, is the tendency to exaggeration and undue vehemence, with the evident intention of producing an immediate effect. There is too much straining after effect, and especially immediate effect. The end sought may be good, unquestionably so, but if the means for its accomplishment have even the appearance of being questionable or strained, the effect will be in large measure, if not totally, destroyed. There should not be a semblance of unfairness in stating a truth, or rebutting an error. The Word of God must not be handled dishonestly, craftily or deceitfully. All exaggeration and lack of candor, or lack of proper discrimination are self-destructive. The moment a preacher produces the impression that he is straining a point to enforce an obligation, he discredits his calling, lowers himself in the esteem of his hearers, does violence to the truth, and most effectually defeats the very object he has in view.

One or two illustrations of what is meant may not be out of place here.

When a preacher states for instance, in order to induce a more regular and constant attendance upon the means of grace, that it is the duty of his hearers to attend church with the same regularity and constancy that he does, he is stating what is manifestly untrue. The obligation is the same up to a certain point, but beyond that it is not the same, in fact it is totally different.

With regard to the duty of worshipping God, and paying proper honor and respect to the place where he has covenanted to meet with his people, the duty is the same: but the preacher is under another obligation, and that is to the church with which he has agreed to perform certain duties, at certain stated times, and for a monetary consideration which is supposed to be agreeable and adequate. He is paid for his attendance; his hearers are not, but rather the reverse; therefore the obligation is not the same, neither can it be accounted equal. It is manifestly and honestly his duty to be there, and ready to perform his appointed task, whether they are or not. And further there may be many valid reasons for their non-attendance which cannot apply to him, but they are too obvious to need mentioning.

It may be as well, perhaps, to mention one. It is the most obvious, and may pass with the least question. Preaching and attendance upon the services of the sanctuary form the main and the most important occupation of the preacher's life. To these, nearly if not quite, he devotes all his thought and strength, and he is enabled to do it by an arrangement to which he is a consenting party.

With the hearer it is totally different. His main occupation, that to which he must devote his thought and strength, is not in the church, but in the world; and if he pursues his vocation honestly, and with the fear of God before his eyes, he is serving God, and subserving his purposes, just as truly as the preacher in the pulpit. Am I excusing wilful negligence of sanctuary duties? By no means. I am simply pleading for common sense, and a fair statement of relative duties.

I once heard a young minister – keen, brilliant, learned, and with a fair endowment of common sense – say to his congregation that neither he nor they had done a thousandth part for God of what they might have done. He was urging with impassioned eloquence, and wonderful vehemence, the duty of a larger liberality when he made the statement: and it is worthy of remark that if ministers ever lose their heads, in an exceptional way, it is liable to be when they are urging people to give more. Now he must have known, upon a moment's consideration, that the statement he made was an exaggeration. The most casual reflection would have told him that there was probably not a single person present, especially himself, who if he gave all he had would give anything like a thousand times more than he had already given, or do a thousand times more than he had already done. In the enthusiasm of the moment he was led, no doubt unconsciously, to sacrifice truth to effect; and yet he failed of the effect too, because it was so clearly manifest that the statement was not in harmony with the probable fact.

In nothing, perhaps, is this tendency to exaggeration

more manifest than in what are called earnest appeals to the unconverted for instant decision. I have been painfully impressed by this fact many a time, and I have pitied the speaker, and pitied the hearers too. Intelligent and Godly earnestness I do not disapprove, but most sincerely and heartily commend.

I honor the man who feels "the burden of souls" upon his heart, and is determined to deliver himself of a fearful responsibility by a plain and faithful deliverance of the Gospel message with which God has intrusted him. Yes, I honor that man, and I know that God will honor him. But the man who steps outside of this plain line of duty, and by mere vociferation, and menace, and crude unintelligent explanations and applications of Scripture, and hell and damnation in abundance, seeks to coerce moral beings, and frighten people into heaven, I have the profoundest contempt

Men must be treated, and have a right to be treated, as reasonable and intelligent beings, and as God always treats them, for He says, "Come let us reason together." If you tell a man he is a sinner, he has a perfect right to ask you to prove it, and you should be ready with your proof. If you tell a man to repent, he has a right to ask you what repentance is, and why he should repent. If you tell a man to believe the Gospel, he has a right to ask you what the Gospel is, and why and how it meets his need. These questions can, and should, be answered reasonably, intelligently, satisfactorily, and with that sweet and persuasive eloquence which should always characterize the ambassador of Jesus Christ. "He that winneth souls is wise."

There is one conspicuously dishonest method of "Handling the Word of God," which is not uncommon with a certain class of preachers. I allude to the plan of taking a text not for the purpose of explaining and endeavoring to show what the mind of the Spirit is, but simply as a peg upon which to hang a number of miscellaneous ideas and observations which have no particular connection, and are certainly not "profitable for doctrine, for reproof, for correction, or for instruction in righteousness."

The most conspicuous example of this method of treating a portion of Scripture I ever heard was on these words, "There shall not a hoof be left behind." A remarkable text indeed, and it was followed not by a remarkable sermon, but by a remarkable series of observations, good, bad, and indifferent, branching out in every conceivable direction. I cannot recall the discourse, if we must for the sake of convenience call it that, for it was of that kind you never can remember, even if your life depended upon it. I recall one thing, however, and that is, that in spite of the prediction the hoof was left behind, for we never heard anything about it until we got to the end of the sermon, when the text was again quoted as a sort of artistic finish, and as a gentle reminder of a supposed connection between it and the discourse.

This is surely not the way to treat the Word of God. No man in his senses can either approve or commend it. It plainly comes within the scope of the Apostle's implied censure, and may be justly called "Walking in craftiness, and handling the Word of God deceitfully." And if ever a man does that consciously and designedly —that is, with a full consciousness and knowledge of what he is doing—it must be because he is not only dishonest but depraved. I speak strongly, but I speak truly. I fail utterly to see how a sane man could bring himself to believe that he could convey any part of the mind and will of God to his hearers from such a text as, "There shall not a hoof be left behind."

Ah! but you say, look at the analogy; contemplate it in its analogical bearings. Yes, I know what you mean, and in answer let me say that analogical preaching is of all preaching the most unsatisfactory and misleading. What is analogy, or rather what is the analogical? It is pointing out certain resemblances that exist, or are supposed to exist, between different things. And if you can find a congregation that is simple enough to accept analogies for arguments, and resemblances for Divine truth, you can prove anything you like to their entire satisfaction. And yet analogy, sparingly and wisely used, may be useful, and to a certain extent is necessary; but it must be distinctly borne in mind that it can never prove anything—it can only illustrate.

Analogical sermons are not difficult to make, and I suppose that is one reason why young preachers, for the most part, fall readily into that kind of preaching.

All that is necessary is to take a portion of Scripture, long or short, but generally short, and get up a list of correspondences or resemblances between certain persons, things, facts, or events, throwing in a few appropriate passages of Scripture, and a few choice anecdotes which will appeal to the sympathies of the hearers, and you have a sermon complete in a short space of time. And I have no doubt that numbers of people will say it is a very nice sermon, and that the preacher is a very nice man, and will go away in the full persuasion that they have been very much edified and blessed. Ah ! those nice sermons and those nice preachers, that send people away well satisfied with themselves, will not, I fear, bear successfully the final analysis and judgment. Suppose you heard somebody call Christ, or John the Baptist, or Peter, or Paul a nice preacher, or their heaven-born deliverances nice sermons, what would you think ? You would think it a most inappropriate description, and you would be perfectly right.

So now, the sermon that is worth hearing, and that will do you lasting good to hear, is not a nice sermon, but a heaven-born deliverance by a heaven-born man that shows forth plainly and clearly the mind and will of God.

And how are such sermons made ? They are made by the gracious help of Almighty God, by the Spirit's endowment, by common sense, by prayer, by patient, earnest, consuming thought, by strong crying and tears, by fighting the good fight of faith and successfully combating doubt and difficulty, by agonizing the excellent agony ; and then, delivered in the same spirit, and by the same aids, they are "Mighty through God."

Let it be distinctly and constantly borne in mind, by those whose special business or calling is "Handling the Word of God," that a sermon may be eloquent, orthodox, learned, scriptural, pleasing, faultlessly delivered, and offending none of the recognized proprieties, and yet it will fail utterly of its real purpose and end unless it stamps upon the minds of the hearers some definite and clear perception of the Divine Will.

The preaching that is needed to meet the requirements of the age is plain, direct, practical, expository preaching. Preaching that contains information of the most important kind, clearly conceived and as clearly expressed. Preaching that is void of whims, fancies, and conceits, and full of unquestioned authority and Divine truth. What the preacher himself thinks is a matter of small account, but what God thinks and what God says, if that can be clearly ascertained, is a matter of paramount importance. Hence we need less exhortation, and more explanation. Less of I think this, and you ought to do that, and more of "Thus saith the

the Lord." Less of exhortation to duty, and more of furnishing adequate motives for the performance of duty in which the Scriptures abound. And you may appeal rightly and successfully to the selfishness, or at least the self-interest of men, for that is sanctioned by the highest authority. As for instance: "For what shall it profit a man, if he shall gain the whole world, and lose his own soul, or what shall a man give in exchange for his soul." Mark 8 ch. 36-37 v. "Godliness is profitable unto all things, having promise of the life that now is, and of that which is to come," 1 Tim. 4 ch. 8 v. "Seek ye first the kingdom of God, and his righteousness, and all these things shall be added unto you," Matt. 6 ch. 33 v. When you have convinced a man, or even partially convinced him, that, as an actual fact and not a mere sentiment, it is more profitable to be Godly than to be ungodly, you have started him in the direction of a moral change which may lead to the entire transformation of his life, and the uplifting of his soul into a higher and purer sphere.

O! thou who standest in the place of Christ, between man and God, think much of His meekness and gentleness, and emulate His example, and drink in His spirit, who did not break the bruised reed, nor quench the smoking flax. Deal gently, and wisely, and reasonably with thy brother man, and he will respond to thy gentleness and wisdom, and follow thee in the way of truth and righteousness. Deal otherwise with him, and he will be repelled. "The servant of the Lord must not strive, but be gentle unto all men, apt to teach, patient, in meekness instructing those that oppose themselves." 2 Tim. 2 ch. 24-25 vs.

These are the qualities needed for successfully commending the truth to the conscience, and bringing men to Christ humility, gentleness, patience, meekness, and aptitude to teach. But it must be confessed, and confessed with shame and confusion of face, that these are not ordinarily the qualities sought for, in a minister of Jesus Christ, by the churches of today. No, they seek youthfulness and immaturity, showiness, a fair exterior, a glib tongue, and especially a minimum of knowledge combined with a maximum of assurance.

Do you say this is a caricature? I wish it was, but unfortunately it is not. Alas! for the cause of Christ it is too true. Why is it not a fact, too well known to be successfully denied, that when a minister has lived, and studied and labored, and suffered long enough to be humble, and gentle, and patient, and meek, and apt to teach, it is discovered that he is too old to be interesting. And not to be interesting, to young people of course, is the unpardonable sin in a minister. His noble weight of years, his ripe experience, his widely extended and varied knowledge, his deep insight into the human heart, his keen analysis of thought, his pathos and his deep sympathy born of years of trial and suffering;—all these are outweighed by that one remarkable defect of not being interesting.

Enough of this. Ring down the curtain. Church of Christ, as thou callest thyself, hide thy face in shame. Alas! for sanctified humanity. "How long, O Lord, how long."

CHAPTER III.

The Inconsistencies of Professing Christians.

WHAT is a Christian? What is a professing Christian What is an inconsistent professing Christian? Three important questions, which if we can answer with a fair show of clearness and satisfaction, we may hope to know just about where we are, and what to do with the caption at the head of this chapter.

What is a Christian? Have you ever thought how widely the ideas of men vary on this matter, and how diverse are their definitions? Any reputable English dictionary will give you several, and almost any man you meet, who is fairly intelligent, will be likely to make a contribution to the already existing list.

One will tell you that a Christian is a civilized being as distinguished from a heathen or a barbarian;

or in other words, an inhabitant of a civilized and Christianized country. Another will tell you that a Christian is one who has been baptized according to the orthodox usage of the church to which he belongs. Another, that he is one who attends church with more or less regularity, and gives of his means for the support of the cause of God. Another, that he is one who has been formally received into the fellowship and membership of the church, having his name duly inscribed upon the roll. Another, that he is a member in good standing of any particular orthodox communion or church. Another, that he is one who is a member of a particular sect or church, outside of which it cannot be allowed that a man can be a Christian at all; for that, it is contended, is the true Church of Christ and there is no other. If I wanted to give a definition, in as few words as possible, it would be this:—a Christian is one who has been born again, believes in Jesus Christ, and follows his Leader.

It is simply amazing to what extent human nature can deceive itself. The intellectual sloth of men, in regard to what pertains to their highest interest and welfare, is almost incredible. They allow themselves to slide and hopelessly sink into merely traditional definitions and beliefs; and hence, there are thousands upon thousands at ease in their consciousness of a possessed Christianity, which no legitimate application of truth or charity could pronounce Christians. It is undeniably so, and this is one of the most cunning, and one of the deepest wiles of the Devil. We have it on the most undoubted authority, that a man may live to the end of his life thinking he is a Christian, die in the full persuasion that he is a Christian, go before the judgment throne, and make a strong appeal to the Judge on the score of the reality and eminence of his Christianity, and yet find that he has been woefully and totally deceived.

This is no vain imagining, for we have it on the authority of Christ himself, and in such positive language that leaves no room for doubt. "Not every one that saith unto me, Lord, Lord, shall enter into the kingdom of heaven, but he that doeth the will of my Father which is in heaven. Many will say to me in that day, Lord, Lord, have we not prophesied in thy name, and in thy name have cast out devils, and in thy name have done many wonderful works? And then will I profess unto them, I never

C

knew you: depart from me, ye that work iniquity." Matt. 7 ch., 21 23 vs.

There can be no doubt about what is meant by the phrase "that day," for it is used in many passages of Scripture besides this, to indicate the great day, the judgment day. "They shall be mine, saith the Lord of hosts, in that day when I make up my jewels," Mal. 3 ch. 17 v. "The Lord grant unto him that he may find mercy of the Lord in that day." 2 Tim. 1 ch. 18 v. Other references might be given to illustrate the point that "that day" means the great day of account, but these are enough for the present purpose. Beside, the reference in Matthew, above quoted, is too plain to be mistaken. Therefore we are confronted by, not simply an awful possibility or probability, but by an awful predicted actuality, that "Many will say unto me in that day," etc.

Clear therefore is it as noonday, and more terrible than any thunder which ever shook the earth, that many can and will cherish a sad delusion with reference to their spiritual state through life, through death, and up to the Judgment throne, which will not be dissipated till they hear the decision which cannot be impeached, and the sentence from which there is no appeal, "I never knew you; depart from me."

The question which settles the reality of your Christianity is, does Christ know you and do you know Him? This then is a very important matter to ascertain, if it can be ascertained, whether Christ knows you and you know Him in that deep spiritual sense which he intended. In other words, whether you are a Christian, that is a Christ's man, and one whom He will recognize and accept in "that day."

There are quite a number of marks or evidences of a Christian in the New Testament, as for instance, love to the brethren—"We know that we have passed from death unto life because we love the brethren;" 1st John, 3 ch., 14 v. It would be tedious to attempt to notice them all, and it is not necessary, because there are three which are fundamental and substantially include all the rest faith, obedience, and moral conformity to Christ.

Faith in Christ is the first. This is the prime requisite, and is the foundation of all that follows. I mean a personal faith in a personal Saviour in order to the personal salvation of the soul. This is something that each one has to attend to for himself. It cannot be delegated to another, neither can it be assumed for another. It is a purely personal matter between the soul and God. Of course a condition of sinfulness, and helplessness in that condition, must be previously recognized as existing, in order to make the reception of so great a gift as salvation necessary and operative. But faith varies, not in nature, but in strength. It may be the firm grasp of a giant upon Christ, or it may be the tender grasp of a little child upon the hem of His garment. I think the reality of faith is the principal test of its value and efficacy.

Then it leads to something else, namely, obedience, which is the second fundamental characteristic of a Christian. He who has a genuine faith in Christ is likely to render an unquestioned and unquestioning obedience to Him in all things. He will not ask useless questions about the reason of this or that, but he will ascertain, as far as he is able, the will of the Master, and then do it without unnecessary delay, and without reservation.

You and I may honestly differ, in our interpretation of the Will of Christ, in some particulars. That is both possible and likely, but we must each follow Christ according to the conviction and light we have, or may attain unto. We must be true to our honest individual interpretations of Christ's will. I am not your master. You are not my master. "For one is your Master even Christ, and all ye are brethren."

The third characteristic follows as logically, and as necessarily, upon the second, as the second upon the first: namely, conformity to the character and life of Christ. Faith in Christ leads to obedience to Him, and obedience to Him culminates in likeness to Him. It is impossible to obey Him without getting into closer sympathy, and an ever increasing moral conformity.

Are these tests reliable? I think they are. The passages of Scripture by which they might be enforced and illustrated are very numerous, and are too obvious to need quoting They will readily occur to any one having even a moderate acquaintance with the New Testament.

Having answered, somewhat at length, the first question at the head of this chapter, the second and third shall be disposed of more briefly.

What is a professing Christian? The answer is simple

and plain. He is one who professes to be and do what we have been endeavoring to describe. He professes to have faith in Christ, to obey Christ in all things, and to be growing daily into the likeness of Christ.

What is an inconsistent professing Christian? Clearly and unmistakably, he is one who, in some degree or measure, is false to his profession, false to his faith, false to his obedience, false to his moral conformity, and therefore false to Christ.

But why all these definitions and explanations, some impatient reader may ask? Well, I like to be frank with you, and I will tell you why. They may be of some use to somebody. Some poor soul not so highly privileged, nor so well informed as you are, may be benefited by a rehearsal of these simple, self-evident truths. Some one who is in doubt and darkness may get a little light, which will give him a clearer apprehension of truths, which are certainly important and fundamental. Or some lone mariner, by this feeble light, may steer his craft clear of the rocks, and get at last into a safe haven. But there is another reason. I have been trying to see that the yard stick is the right length, because I am going to make an attempt to measure somebody, perhaps you, and I want to be strictly honest. I don't want to be unfair, neither do I wish to take any unfair advantage.

Or to change the simile, to illustrate the same idea, I have been trying the balance to make as sure as a poor fallible mortal can that it is all right. I want to give you your just weight:

> "Nothing extenuate
> Nor set down aught in malice."

Surely you will admire my good intentions, whatever you may say of my performances when you weigh them in your balance.

And then thirdly, as the preachers say, how can I tell you, or even pretend to tell you, what is inconsistent in a Christian, until I have first settled, as well as I can, what he ought to be and do, according to the highest standard, and the most undoubted authority. No, clearly, what has been already put down here is necessary in order to execute the remainder of our task with proper discrimination and justice, and in such a way that he who may get hit, and perhaps hit badly, may at least confess that he has not been treated unfairly.

One thing may safely be taken for granted, confirmed

as it is by undisputed facts and a large experience, that there is no argument for Christianity so convincing as a consistent Christian life; and there is no argument against it so weighty and overwhelming as an inconsistent one; hence, the fearful responsibility resting upon all who bear the Christian name, and make a Christian profession. Men of the world may neglect the Bible, and leave it upon the shelf unused and forgotten, but they do not neglect to observe and study the lives of professing Christians. Whether they are competent judges may be seriously doubted, but they are judges nevertheless; and they should be able to see in a Christian some reflection of the Divine Will as clear, though not as full and perfect, as they might, if they were so minded, read it in the Written Word. This is plainly what the apostle means in Rom. 12 ch. 2 v. where he says, " Be not conformed to this world, but be ye transformed by the renewing of your mind, that ye may prove" that is, that ye may show forth, manifest

"what is that good, and acceptable, and perfect will of God."

I wish to introduce here, before I forget, some observations about that common, oft-repeated charge of inconsistency in ministers in accepting calls to larger salaries. We have heard it so often that it has become stale and unprofitable. Is there anything in it? Not much; certainly not near so much as some unfriendly critics imagine. There would be nothing in it at all if ministers displayed more common sense, and would be more honest in their pretensions and statements. I have come to the conclusion, after a good deal of thought, and I might add a good deal of painful experience, that while the call to preach the Gospel must be admitted to be a Divine call, the call to exercise the gift for the exclusive benefit of any particular community or church is largely, if not wholly, a human arrangement: the desirability or otherwise of which should be decided by considerations based upon circumstances, reason and common sense.

I am willing to admit the reality of the headship of Jesus Christ, and what seems to logically follow from that admission; but I confess it passes my comprehension how to associate the honored name, "which is above every name," with the ordinary circumstances and methods, attendant upon calling and uncalling ministers, which are well known to exist in many churches of to-day. It seems to be the maxim of some churches, at least of some people in them, to reverse the apostolic injunction, "Neither give place to the devil;" and this would appear to exemplify itself in a marked degree in the matter of settling and unsettling ministers. I therefore feel myself irresistibly drawn, by the logic of facts, and by a scrupulous regard for the untarnished honor of the Great Head of the church, to come to the conclusion, that while the call to preach is divine, and must ever be maintained as such, the call to occupy any particular sphere is human, and therefore a business arrangement.

Will any man seriously contend that the Divine Man could even remotely, or by implication, give His sanction to the calling of a minister to two or three churches at the same time, which is notoriously the case in some instances we have heard of? Are such calls Divine calls? We know they are not. No stretch of human credulity can make them such. Therefore if ministers and churches would throw away their nonsense, and come down to plain sense, the charge against the former of worldliness and inconsistency in accepting larger salaries would instantly vanish. Why? Because it would cease to apply, for any reasonable man would admit that, on the basis suggested, a minister has the same right as any other man to make the most of his abilites for himself, his family, and the future of both, without sacrificing conscience, truth, or his loyalty to God.

Having disposed of this matter, I hope with some measure of conviction and satisfaction, —let us look now at the question of wealth, its responsibilities, duties and failures, from a Christian standpoint. Charity and truth suggest that there are some wealthy men who are Christians, known to be such not only by their profession, but by their deeds. By their fruits they are known. Also, there are doubtless a great many of that class who, at least, make some sort of a profession of Christianity, and who would feel very much hurt if you cast any doubt upon the reality of that profession ; and there are others who would scarcely be affected at all by your opinion concerning them. I confess that with all the charity I can bring to bear, a very wealthy Christian, while I do not deny his possible existence, is a puzzle to me. I don't understand him. I find myself looking at him with wistful, doubting eyes. I cannot help thinking of what Christ said: "How hardly shall they that have riches enter into the Kingdom of God," showing clearly that the rich man is likely to have a hard time of it when he attempts to go in the direction of the kingdom, with that large pack of accumulated wealth on his back. He may get in—Christ does not say he will not—but his case would be a good deal less problematical and doubtful, and he would move along with a quicker, firmer, lighter step, if he would take off that precious pack, and distribute its contents, at least a part of them, to those who are ready to perish, and who would live to bless his name.

And then I cannot help thinking of that terrible picture which the Divine Artist has drawn, with a master hand, in which He puts aside the invisible veil, and lets us look for a moment into the next world. If I wanted to invent a name for that picture, I would call it This and That. The main figure in it is a certain man. Not a bad man, according to the generally accepted meaning of the word, but simply a 'rich man; a man well housed, well clothed, and well fed every day of his life. He had the best of everything, and simply enjoyed himself, as he thought he had a right to do with his own. What did he care about the poor man at his gate? The dogs could take care of him, and they did. Wealth could not purchase immunity from death. He must pay the debt of nature. He died, and then, O horrors ! what a change when he lifted up his eyes, and saw where he was. Why this ? What had he done ? Simply lived for himself, and neglected his plain duty to God and his fellow men. Simply did what thousands of his class are doing to-day, and some of them are in our churches, and they call themselves Christians. Christians! and professed followers of Him who " though he was rich, yet for your sakes he became poor, that ye through his poverty might be rich."

My rich brother, does it not strike you as a very grave inconsistency, that you should profess to be daily striving after a likeness to Him who literally emptied Himself to fill other people, while you are concerned about how to make and to keep. He distributed of His abundant resources, even to the extent of giving His life, while you are not happy unless you see your precious pile of wealth increasing day by day. And then you profess to believe in the Bible, and accept its teaching as the guide of your life, and it tells you plainly that "you are not your own," and if not your own how can what you have be yours. And then you are told "to lay not up for yourself treasures upon earth, but to lay up for yourself treasures in heaven." And how can you lay up treasures for yourself in heaven? By using and distributing your wealth, according to the will of Him who owns you and the wealth too. You will then become rich toward God.

And then what about those men and women, and boys and girls, in your factories, and workshops, and stores? Do you look upon them as real flesh and blood, as human beings, as brothers and sisters in the flesh, and perhaps in the spirit too; as members of the one common brotherhood of which you form a part? Or do you follow the wake of the world and worldly craft, and enterprise, and account them as so much raw material out of which to manufacture wealth? Which is it? They know you profess to be a Christian, and they expect to see you act like one; and it will be a glad and joyful, and even profitable thing for them if you do. Well, you say, I conduct my business on business principles. You do? Well, I suppose you really mean that you conduct it on the same principles as a fairly honest man does who makes no profession of Christianity. Or in other words, your Christianity is not taken into account, nor does it appear in your business at all. You think you have done your duty when you have done what other people are doing, under like conditions, who do not profess what you do. Do you call that consistency? Can you call it honesty? Can you really persuade yourself that it is common sense? I have a better opinion of you than to suppose you can.

As a Christian you are bound to conduct your business on Christian principles, that is, according to the law of Christ, for you are commanded "to let your light so shine before men, that they may see your good works, and glorify your Father which is in heaven." And if your light does not shine in your business, where is it going to shine; for it is in that you grind out your life daily and show unmistakably what you are.

But, you say, I must do as other people do, else I shall not be able to successfully compete with them. Not so my brother. You must not do as other people do, except so far as they do right. You must do what Christ, your rightful Lord and Master, bids you do. What, in my business? Yes, in your business. But I can never make it a success on that line, and people will laugh at me, and say I am very peculiar, and all that. Well, let them laugh, and remember there is a saying to the effect that he laughs best who laughs last.

But I can never succeed on that line, because competition is keen, and the majority of people—I might say nearly all of them —are working on the other line. Then give up your business or calling, and try to find something, the working of which will not conflict with your high and sacred profession. But I cannot do that either, for it is my living, my all in this world. Well then, be honest and give up your Christianity, or at least your profession of it. Come, settle this business as you should settle it. Face the alternative and decide. Be a man. Give up that wretched, abortive attempt at being a man of the world and a Christian at the same time, which is being no man at all. Either strike your colors and doff your regimentals, or toe the mark, and stand straight up a full, honest, consistent Christian man before God and the world.

I hear some one whisper, that man is a crank. Well, what is a crank? A crank, in a general way, is something crooked, twisted ; and in these days it has come to be applied in a variety of connections by people of limited ideas and of a limited vocabulary.

It is certainly a misnomer as far as I am concerned, for I am contending, all along the line, for what is straight, as opposed to what is crooked.

But you say it is a high and impossible ideal of Christian consistency and duty I am setting up. Do you think so? Allow me to inform you that it is no ideal at all, but something practical and practicable, and certainly consistent, and you know consistency is a jewel. And you rich Christians and employers of labor must try to get the notion of ideality out of your heads, and try to see that business upon Christian principles is consistent and practicable, and can be made actual, to the manifest advantage of men, and to the Glory of God. Failing this, notwithstanding your profession, the day of reckoning will come, when the prediction of the centuries will be fulfilled in your bitter experience :—" Go to now, ye rich men, weep and howl for your miseries that shall come upon you. Your riches are corrupted and your garments are moth-eaten. Your gold and silver is cankered, and the rust of them shall be a witness against you, and shall eat your flesh as it were fire : ye have heaped treasure together for the last days. Behold, the hire of the laborers who have reaped down your fields, which is of you kept back by fraud, crieth ; and the cries of them which have reaped are entered in the ears of the Lord of Sabaoth. Ye have lived in pleasure on the earth, and been wanton ; ye have nourished your hearts as in a day of slaughter. Ye have condemned and killed the just, and he doth not resist you." James 5 ch. 1-6 vs.

A glaring inconsistency, which scarcely any one can fail to notice, is the undue value attached to wealth, and the commanding influence exercised by men of wealth in the churches of to day. There are two things of which we may feel morally certain in regard to this matter.

The first is, the small value that God attaches to wealth ; the second is, the great value attached to it by the churches. Any one will be convinced of the soundness and truth of the first proposition by carefully reading Christ's sermon on the mount, especially that part of it beginning with : "Therefore I say unto you, take no thought for your life," etc. The spiritual is of paramount importance, and is worthy of our highest regard, and unceasing care, while the material is not worth the thought ordinarily bestowed upon it. Hence, "Seek ye first"— first in point of importance as well as time—" the Kingdom of God and His righteousness, and all these things shall be added unto you." The things to be added are food and raiment, and all necessary material things, which as compared with the spiritual are of small value indeed. As to the second proposition, the great importance attached to wealth in the church and by the church, it is self-evident and indisputable, to any who have eyes to see, ears to hear, and understanding enough to understand.

Go into any church, I mean any community of Christians, and you will soon find out that the men of commanding position and influence, who mainly decide what shall be done and what shall not be done, are not the men eminent for piety, and poor, as such generally are, but the men of wealth and social position. There may be an exception here and there, and I hope for the credit of the church there is, but I cannot honestly say that I ever met one. Now, this is all wrong; it is manifestly inconsistent; it is at variance with the will of the Master; it is reversing the proper order of things which ought to exist in a Christian church, and it ought to be trampled upon, and stamped out as speedily as possible.

Do not misunderstand me. I dislike being misunderstood, and it shall not be if I can avoid it. I do not say that there may not be some men in a church eminent for wealth and piety too; and I do not say that they should not have their just recognition and influence which their possessions, lawfully acquired and generously used, fairly entitle them to.

But I do say, and will maintain with my latest breath, that wealth alone, without regard to the methods of its acquirement and use, and without regard to qualifications of a spiritual nature, does not entitle its possessor to distinguished position and influence in a Christian church.

It is singular, and worthy of observation, how these inconsistencies, which we have been commenting upon, and others that might be mentioned, all spring from, or are connected with, or cluster around that one word, money. It is only another way of saying that they spring from conformity to the world, and worldly maxims and customs. There is that matter of dress, for instance, which helps to intensify and perpetuate discrimination against the poor as such. It is a difficult matter to touch, and a very delicate one, and a wise man, however much he may deplore the evil, finds himself unable to say much about it. And especially will he hesitate, and distrust himself, in view of the fact that he most pungent dissertation ever given, about invidious distinctions in the house of God, based upon difference in dress and worldly estate, was given eighteen hundred years ago. and as far as can be seen with little or no effect.

"My brethren, have not the faith of our Lord Jesus Christ, the Lord of glory, with respect of persons. For if there come into your assembly a man with a gold ring, in goodly apparel, and there come in also a poor man in vile raiment ; and ye have respect unto him that weareth the gay clothing, and say unto him, sit thou here in a good place, and say to the poor, stand thou there, or sit here under my footstool. Are ye not then partial in yourselves, and are become judges of evil thoughts? Hearken. my beloved brethren, hath not God chosen the poor of this world rich in faith, and heirs of the kingdom which he hath promised to them that love him? But ye have despised the poor. Do not rich men oppress you, and draw you before the judgment seats? Do not they blaspheme that worthy name by the which ye are called? If ye fulfil the royal law according to the scripture, thou shalt love thy neighbor as thyself, ye do well. But if ye have respect to persons, ye commit sin, and are convinced of the law as transgressors. For whosoever shall keep the whole law and yet offend in one point, he is guilty of all." James 2 ch. 1-10 vs.

While things may not be quite so bad now, in this respect, as they evidently were in apostolic times, it is undeniable that this spirit of invidious worldliness is not altogether extinct. Distinctions are made, lines are drawn, significant looks are exchanged, remarks are made, and the poor are offended. It must be apparent, even to the casual observer, that a man of good social position, and ample means, making his advent into a Christian community, is received quite cordially, and even effusively; while a poor man, however high up intellectually and spiritually, is received quite formally and with discrimination.

Again I may be misunderstood if I don't put in one of my parenthetical explanations. Do I object to the rich man being received cordially, and if you like effusively? I do not, but you might as well spare your exuberance—he will not miss it, and may not be worthy of it—and bestow it upon the poor man who may be cheered by it, and will certainly appreciate it if it be transparently sincere. Do you know where the inconsistency of this discrimination against the poor as such comes in?

It comes in just here, that it is totally opposed to the spirit, will and conduct of Jesus Christ. Have you ever given the matter a really serious thought? If you have not, do so now, and you will find it will bear the closest investigation, and the severest scrutiny you can bring to bear upon it. You will find that not wealth, nor position, nor loud professions of exceptional saintliness, but character was the coin which passed current with Jesus Christ. You will find also that the severer aspects of His character and demeanor, His unbending sternness and His withering denunciations, were invariably manifested to and hurled against the proud, the opulent, and the wealthy, the men of commanding influence and undoubted position in church and State. But to the poor and lowly He invariably showed the tenderest aspect of His infinitely tender nature, and spoke to them and of them kindly, gently, and manifested toward them a remarkable patience, and a loving consideration. He was always ready to take up their cause and defend them as He alone could, unmasking their oppressors, and launching upon them His fierce invective and blighting scorn.

Bear in mind that in making these statements, concerning Christ, I am not indulging in hyperbole, or exaggerating facts for the purpose of making out a case. I am stating in strong, but not too strong, language what you and I, who have read the life of Christ as recorded in the gospels, know to be true.

As an illustration of Christ's severity to certain classes take the whole of the twenty-third chapter of Matthew, of which a part only shall be quoted here: "But woe unto you, Scribes and Pharisees, hypocrites! for ye shut up the kingdom of heaven against men; for ye neither go in yourselves, neither suffer ye them that are entering to go in. Woe unto you, Scribes and Pharisees, hypocrites! for ye devour widows' houses, and for a pretence make long prayers; therefore ye shall receive the greater damnation. Woe unto you, Scribes and Pharisees, hypocrites! for ye compass sea and land to make one proselyte, and when he is made, ye make him two-fold more the child of hell than yourselves. Woe unto you, Scribes and Pharisees, hypocrites! for ye pay tithe of mint and anise and cummin, and have omitted the weighter matters of the law, judgment, mercy and faith : these ought ye to have done, and not to leave the other undone. Ye blind guides, which strain at a gnat, and swallow a camel. Woe unto you, Scribes and Pharisees, hypocrites! for ye are like unto whited sepulchres, which indeed appear beautiful outward, but are within full of dead men's bones, and of all uncleanness. Even so ye also outwardly appear righteous unto men, but within ye are full of hypocrisy and iniquity. Ye serpents, ye generation of vipers, how can ye escape the damnation of hell."

As illustrations of Christ's tenderness and compassion and care for the poor, the unfortunate, the heavy laden, and the defenceless, take those deeply heartfelt utterances of His commencing with "Come unto me ;" or the parable of the good Samaritan, which answers that world-wide but much neglected question, "Who is my neighbor?" or that plain statement concerning the proper direction, and the fitting objects of generosity and hospitality recorded in Luke 14 ch. 12 14 vs. "Then said he also to him that bade him, when thou makest a dinner or a supper, call not thy friends, nor thy brethren, neither thy kinsmen, nor thy rich neighbors, lest they also bid thee again, and a recompense be made thee. But when thou makest a feast, call the poor, the maimed, the lame, the blind; and thou shalt be blessed, for they cannot recompense thee; for thou shalt be recompensed at the resurrection of the just."

We must bear in mind that this language is not figurative, but absolutely literal: as literal as that two and two make four. It has been on record for about eighteen hundred years, and comes with unquestioned authority, and from the Divinest source. There can be no doubt that it was intended to have an important bearing upon one aspect of the social life of the followers of Christ, and to teach a practical lesson of priceless worth, the connection between the conduct of the present and the blessed fruition of the future. How many are practising it? Indeed, are there any who treat the matter seriously at all, or even give it a transient thought. Not many I fear, certainly it is not general.

It is so uncommon, so universally recognized as being against the proprieties to ask people to visit you and partake of your substantials who are not of your set, but are beneath you in social position, that if, by chance, you should see some good simple minded Christian consistently carrying out the plain directions of his Master, he would be put down as a crank, and that is the next thing to being called a lunatic. Then, why is this? You cannot successfully dispute the literality of the exhortation, or doubt the sincerity of Jesus Christ. He meant just what He said. Then, why don't you as a professed follower of Him attend to it, and please Him by a literal and prompt obedience? O! you say, I think you are making too much of it, and forgetting that "the letter killeth, but the spirit giveth life." Well, suppose you try to extract the spirit or principle, and see what it looks like. I think you will see that it comes to the same thing exactly, namely, the necessity of shaping your conduct in this particular not according to the usages of the world, but according to the well-known leanings and preferences of the Master you profess to love and serve.

Of course, if you do this, people will say that you are

peculiar, very peculiar, and with a very peculiar emphasis upon very; but you will have the satisfaction of feeling and knowing that you are consistent and loyal; and even they will scarcely be able to refrain from honoring you for your consistency and loyalty. And then think how the poor will bless you for your love and goodness, and think of the reward—"thou shalt be recompensed at the resurrection of the just."

I propose to stop here. I have not exhausted the list, and had no intention of doing so when I commenced writing this chapter. Exhaustiveness is liable to end in exhaustion, and that is not pleasant. It would take a volume to cover the whole ground, but that is neither desirable nor necessary. Quite a number of inconsistencies, call them little if you like, crop up constantly, and are matters of common observation—these are too obvious to need mentioning. The gross, flagrant ones, that are aired in the public prints, and that make people stare and talk, for nine days at least, shall not be advertised in these pages. They get all the publicity they are entitled to.

One thing more. If, as a follower of Jesus Christ, you are sincerely desirous of leading a consistent life, you must pay small heed to the world, and much to your Leader. And you had better keep in mind this apostolic exhortation and the rich promise attached: "Wherefore come out from among them, and be ye separate saith the Lord, and touch not the unclean; and I will receive you, and will be a Father unto you, and ye shall be my sons and daughters, saith the Lord Almighty," 2nd Cor., 6 ch., 17, 18 vs.

CHAPTER IV.

Church Methods and Work.

THE present chapter is likely to cover a wide field of observation, involving matters of the most practical kind, and requiring a fair amount of knowledge and skill in their proper treatment. Any one, to speak with advantage, and with some measure of authority, upon Church Methods and Work, should have occupied different points of vantage ground for observation, and should be able to speak clearly, truthfully and charitably. He must not be afraid to tell what he has seen and knows, and yet he must not forget that the best of men are human, and some of them intensely so.

It is one thing to look at the church and its workings from the pulpit; it is quite another thing to make your observations from the pew. He who observes exclusively from either the one or the other, is likely to come to a partially erroneous and unsatisfactory conclusion. I claim the advantage of making my observations from both points of view.

I have, at different periods of my life, occupied the one position, and then the other, and had the privilege of criticising the pew from the pulpit, and the pulpit from the pew : and from this dual position I propose to record my observations, for the benefit of any who may choose to "read, mark, learn, and inwardly digest." I suppose it is scarcely necessary to warn you that I shall not shrink from stating the naked truth as it appears to me. I ask no man's favor : I fear no man's frown. I seek the favor of God, and hope to obtain it by a strict adherence to truth and charity. Truth and charity did I say? Yes, these are my attendant angels. By the aid of the one I shall mark keenly : by the aid of the other I shall record my judgments as leniently as the limits of truth will allow. Even then they may appear harsh to some people, but remember that the harshness of truth is really a blessing. "Faithful are the wounds of a friend," and truth though sometimes wounding is always a friend.

The most important and the most conspicuous

worker, in any individual church, is the minister, or pastor, or whatever else you choose to call him. Names, in this connection, are quite immaterial. However titles may differ in designating men occupying the same office, and doing the same work, minister is an appropriate designation in any or all of them, for their vocation is to minister to the spiritual necessities of others. I say the minister is the most important and the most conspicuous worker. On him, under God, much depends, and round him cluster all the forces, for good or evil, which issue from the individual community of which he is the recognized head.

The power of appointment varies. It may be with the Bishop, as in the Catholic and Anglican churches. It may be with the Stationing Committee, representing the Conference, as in the Methodist Church. It may be the congregation, with the concurrence of the Presbytery, as in the Presbyterian body. Or it may be with the church absolutely, as in the Baptist and Congregational bodies. In any case a deep responsibility rests upon the appointing power, for much depends upon fitness to secure success.

It is worthy of remark in passing, that the Anglican

and Methodist bodies are drifting in the direction of a more democratic form of government, especially in the matter of allowing the people a larger power in the selection of their ministers. This is doubtless a movement in the right direction, although, as we know, there are evils connected with a pure democracy. But whether the appointing power is with the Bishop, or the Stationing Committee, or the Presbytery in conjunction with the congregation, or with the church itself, Is the question of fitness, between the minister and the charge assigned to him, sufficiently considered? Is it the prime consideration? It is supposed to be so, but is it so, in every case, or in a majority of cases? I am told that he who stands best with the Bishop is likely to get the best appointment. I am told that there is a good deal of wire-pulling, and consequent heart-burning, at Conference; and that he who has friends at court is likely to come off best. These things I have been told, and I give the information as it has come to me, and without exaggeration; and you are quite at liberty to adopt your own method of estimating its value. But with reference to the Presbyterian, and Baptists, and Congregationalists I can speak more positively ; for I know there is a good deal of self-seeking, and the question of fitness is frequently left far in the rear.

What is fitness? Before I answer that question I want to put a few questions on this matter, because I think the answers that would probably be given will go a long way towards showing that fitness, in the true application of that word, is about the last thing that is seriously thought of in a general way. You can suppose the questions addressed to different congregations, or churches, that are pastorless ; and who are therefore presumably looking for the right men, according to their ideas, to fill the vacancies.

What are the qualifications you are looking for in your future minister?

Well, we must have a man who will suit the young people. That is absolutely necessary. We have a large number, and unless we get a minister who will suit them they will wander off to other churches and be lost to us.

But what about the middle aged, and the elder people in your congregation? Do they not merit some consideration?

Well, we don't mind so much about them. They can

get along anyhow, and so long as the young people are suited they will be satisfied. Beside many of them are getting considerably advanced in life, and will die off in a few years, but the young are likely to remain, and they are the hope of the future you know.

But what do you mean by getting a man to suit the young people? What sort of a man must he be? I suppose you have a conception, or perhaps an ideal?

Well, he must be young, the younger the better.

He must be interesting; have taking, pleasant, agreeable ways with him; be quite familiar, and shake hands all round, and play with the boys and girls, call them by short names, such as Tom, Dick, Harry, Jane, Mary, etc. Why, bless you, young people always like a young minister. It's natural you know. Yes, I see you are going a good deal on the natural, and not much on the spiritual.

Will it ever occur to any one, with sufficient force to lead to some practical result, that perhaps this perpetual desire to please young people in the selection of ministers, which obtains in some churches, is being carried altogether too far. Is the object aimed at really definite and worthy? Are they the best judges, and if not why the allowance of a preponderating influence in so important a matter? That it is best for them may be seriously questioned. That it is unfair to the elder part of the community may be presumed to be self-evident. That it is injurious to the real interests of the church, experience abundantly testifies.

And that it leads to a gross injustice to a large number of worthy, efficient ministers, who unfortunately for them are no longer accounted young, cannot be denied. This craze for young ministers to suit young people, and a few older ones who are still very immature, is being carried too far, and should be stamped out. You have heard of the dead line of fifty in the ministry? If you don't happen to know what it means let me enlighten your ignorance by telling you. It doesn't mean that a minister is dead at fifty, but it means that he might just as well be dead as far as his chances for getting a call are concerned, if he happens to need one. That is what it means unless he is one of a thousand who by extraordinary talents or exceptional good fortune has escaped the general doom. These things ought not so to be. You never think that years, and experience, and knowledge, and wisdom are disqualifications in the professions of law and medicine. Then why in the highest of all callings where these qualities are so imperatively required. The very best work can be done by the most experienced ministers if you give them a fair chance.

But suppose we address a question to a leading brother connected with quite a different congregation.

What sort of a minister are you expecting to get? What qualifications, etc.?

Well, nothing but the finest man that can be got will suit us. You see our congregation is quite aristocratic. The best people socially and intellectually attend with us, consequently we must have a minister of undoubted refinement and culture. We must feel that he is unquestionably one who will not, in private or in public, offend any of the recognized proprieties. He must be a perfect gentleman in every sense of the word : one who can go into the most select company, and always be a credit to us. And then in preaching he must have choice thoughts, a refined manner, and a strictly correct pronunciation. Not too much voice, a little emphasis, but no gesticulation, or next to none, and he must avoid all excess and urgency. We don't want to have one's nerves shocked by what some people call earnestness, which in some preachers is liable to degenerate into vulgarity. In short, the man we want must be of finished education, eminently judicious, and thoroughly refined in tone and manner.

Perhaps by far the largest number of pastorless churches are looking out for the man who can make a great hit, and create a sensation. One who can fill the church with a gaping crowd, and may-be, lift a handsome debt, and re-fill an empty treasury. I pity the man who accepts a call, or is appointed to a church with such plans and expectations. In a large percentage of cases disappointment will ensue, and the end will be not far off.

Having disposed of these hypothetical cases, which may be taken as fairly representative of the actual, I propose to answer the question, What is fitness, and what are the qualities that should be sought for in a minister of Jesus Christ? First you are justified in requiring that he shall have the ordinary evidences of being a converted man. Well, all ministers are converted, are they not?

I wish they were, but human experience, and observation, and incontrovertible facts suggest that probably they are not. Indeed, there have been some notable instances of this kind. Have you not heard or read that the celebrated Dr. Chalmers was, upon his own confession, an unconverted man for several years after his induction into the ministry, and the pastoral charge of a church? And if Dr. Chalmers could be mistaken in so vital a matter it is not unreasonable to suppose that other and lesser men may be. I am not referring now to men who designedly try to pass themselves off as Christians when they know they are not, but to those who are genuinely, from whatever cause, deceived in regard to their true spiritual state. This is clearly and plainly possible, hence the necessity for circumspection and close analysis.

If you want to make as sure as you can that you are getting a converted man to fill your pulpit, you must pay small heed to rich, ambitious worldly men, who because of their riches and social position, and not because of any exceptionally keen spiritual discernment, seek to exercise paramount influence in such matters.

You must also depend less upon certificates of membership, character, and standing: recommendations by distinguished ministers, and especially reports of past achievements and brilliant successes, which have appeared from time to time in the columns of religious periodicals and papers. And always be careful about reports of a man receiving many and very distinguished calls.

Again I say don't depend so much upon these things, but place some reliance upon your plain common sense, and powers of observation, and spiritual insight. Then if you are in any doubt, and want a reference, go to some experienced Christian, who, though poor in this world, is rich in faith. One whose worldly position may be nothing, or next to nothing; but who is godly to the very core, varied and wide in experience, mighty in the Scriptures, and deeply imbued with the Spirit of God. He will be a safer guide than your rich neighbor or brother, however much he may vaunt his piety, or display his liberality

Not only have you a right to expect that your minister shall be a converted man, but you are warranted in looking for certain distinguished personal qualities, fitting him for his work in the pulpit and out of it. What are they? We surely cannot be wrong if we say that they are those set forth eighteen hundred years ago, in a letter written by an old minister, putting off the harness, to a young minister who was just putting it on, —the aged Paul to young Timothy, his son in the faith. What he has to say should carry considerable weight, for it springs alike from inspiration, from a large and varied experience, and from a genuine regard and affection for the young man to whom the letter was addressed. Here is what he says, "The servant of the Lord must not strive, but be gentle unto all men, apt to teach, patient; in meekness instructing," etc. 2 Tim. 2 ch. 24-25 vs. You have to bear in mind that he is the Lord's servant, and he must keep it in mind too, for therein the responsibility is properly estimated and fixed; and let no man interfere with it.

He must not strive. He is not a man of war, but a man of peace. His message is peace, and his mission too. He must not cultivate a contentious spirit, but the opposite. He must not allow himself to be drawn into contention, nor kept in it. But there is a limit, and the limit is truth, or principle, or loyalty to God. When he is pushed there, by the devil or his agents, and peace is demanded on such terms as involve a sacrifice of truth or loyalty, he must resist, and if need be, in the strength of God, fight to a finish. The not striving, or avoiding, by all lawful means, occasions of strife, shows a peaceful and humble spirit, and humility should characterise a servant of the Lord. Gentleness is another admirable and necessary feature, and "gentle unto all men," showing that it is not assumed for extraordinary occasions, or for a select few. He is to be patient too, and he must cultivate meekness. He needs both, and fortunate for him, and for others, if he has them in an eminent degree.

But there is another qualification, and probably the most important one, "Apt to teach." That means that he must be able to teach, that he must like teaching, that he must have a peculiar aptitude and readiness in teaching; and that he must regard teaching as a very important and necessary part of his work, without which all the rest will not amount to much.

But perhaps the most practical and the most important meaning which may, at least inferentially, be attached to the phrase is that teaching is the most important part of preaching. In other words, that teaching is preaching, and preaching should be mainly teaching. An eminently able and fearless man has said, and said truly, "As the principal business of a preacher of the Gospel is to teach, or to communicate to his fellow-men the knowledge of the truth, the necessity of this qualification is obvious. No one should be allowed to enter the ministry who is not qualified to impart instruction to others on the doctrines and duties of religion; and no one should feel that he ought to continue in the ministry, who has not industry, and self-denial and the love of study enough to lead him constantly to endeavor to increase in knowledge, that he may be qualified to teach others. A man who would teach a people, must himself keep in advance of them on the subjects on which he would instruct them." These are brave words, and wise. They have the true ring. They come from a veteran watchman on the walls of Zion. They have a discriminating, dividing quality, and are like a two edged sword striking at the entrance, and striking into the ranks. True it is, and indisputable, that no man should be allowed to enter the ministry unless he has evident qualifications for teaching others; and true is it also that no man should remain in the ministry unless he is a growing man, and increasingly answers to that terse description of a capable minister, "Apt to teach."

Now sum up these qualities or qualifications, and look at them fairly and squarely, and what have we? We have a truly converted man who is humble, gentle, patient, meek, and able and apt in teaching others. These are the qualities you have a right to expect in the occupant of your pulpit, whether actual or prospective.

Are you looking for them, or for the man in whom they inhere, or are you looking for something altogether different? Are you measuring the candidates that come before you to preach their trial sermons by this Divine standard, or by some other standard which you have set up; or perhaps by a dozen different standards set up by a dozen different cliques contained in the one, supposed to be, united church?

How is it? You are supposed to follow the King's leading, and act in the King's spirit, and obey the King's commands. Are you doing that, or are you following out your own little petty schemes and devices; and trying to thwart some other brother, or some sister church, that is plotting and scheming as you are? Which is it? I am not a rich man, but I will undertake to give a reward of unmentioned nature and value to the man who will point me out a church whose officers and members, when seeking a minister, deliberately set to work to guide themselves in their choice by the New Testament model, and by those requirements and qualities set forth in Paul's letters to Timothy.

You think there is something odd and whimsical about this proposition, and you may be right, but underneath, if you will look, there is a deep seriousness which you cannot fail to see. If what is, in the strongest manner, implied by the proposition be true, it reveals a lamentable state of things, and goes very far to show the fundamental cause of many things which weaken and disgrace our churches. How can the most important engagement, into which a church can enter, be right, or continue right, or end right if the beginning is wrong. Whether a minister shall serve a particular church, on the basis of certain important and necessary considerations, may be largely a business arrangement; but whether the church has a right to call him and he to accept at all is dependent, or should be dependent, not upon personal likes or dislikes, but upon his manifest and undoubted fitness for the position according to the

New Testament standard. And the churches that do not choose their ministers, where they have the chance of choice, according to that standard fail in their loyalty to Christ, and are neither consulting nor subserving their own best interests.

It is time to consider now how you should treat your minister when you have secured him. What ought to be the demeanor, and what are the duties of the church to him, its chosen head? Unfortunately these things are, for the most part, regulated by what were the dominant ideas of the dominant men in the church when the pastor was called. He, poor man, in the simplicity of his heart, probably supposed that the church in calling him was following the directions given in the inspired text book, and that he was chosen because he was thought to possess the qualities therein described; but he finds out, after a while, that other and totally different considerations decided the case. Hence the ecclesiastical machine gets out of gear from the start, and smoothness in the running of it becomes an utter and palpable impossibility. O! when will men and churches get to be honest in this business? All sorts of trouble, and disappointment, and heart burning, and failure would be avoided by it, to the manifest advantage of all concerned.

If you want a minister not after the New Testament model be frank enough to say so. If you want one simply to lift a mortgage, or replenish an empty treasury; or to fill some big empty galleries, which stare you out of countenance, and make you shiver every time you look at them; or to be pleasant and agreeable all round, dancing attendance upon everybody; or to be quite æsthetic so as not to offend your refined tastes; or to be able to work in perfect harmony with some overbearing ambitious brother who wants to rule the church and the minister too;—if you want a minister for any or all of these purposes be kind enough and honest enough to tell him so, and then he will know what to do. He will at least know whether he is dealing with honest people, and with a Christian church.

But need you be in any doubt as to what is due to him from the church as its pastor and as the servant of Jesus Christ? I think not. Without going into detail, which would be tedious, let me say that if you are satisfied you have, not a perfect man, but a good man, a converted man, a true Christian man: a man who is humble without being servile; gentle, without being weak; meek, without being tame; patient, without being irresolute and sluggish; and fully able to give you instruction in the doctrines and duties of Christianity; —if you have such a man, he is worthy of all the respect and honor you can pay him, and all the support you can bestow upon him. With such a man you cannot be too generous with your good will, your esteem, your confidence, or your money. It will all come back to you in real blessing, and a hundred fold.

At the same time, don't be so foolish as to expect to agree with him in everything. He does not expect it, neither should you. You should accord him all deserving honor, and all needed support, not in proportion as he may happen to fall in with your ideas and please you, but in proportion as he is faithful to his high and sacred trust.

Yes, I say faithful, and I use the word advisedly, and with a definite purpose and meaning. There is too much worshipping the god of success to-day, and too much discount on fidelity. It is fidelity that God honors, and will honor, and not success; and it is fidelity and not success that should be honored in the servants of God, by the church of God. And further it is fidelity that the servants of God should aim at as their highest ambition and chief glory, and not the attainment of success, however complete and distinguished.

And yet, what are the facts, the melancholy facts? That ministers and churches have alike gone clean mad on this subject of success; and it has led, and is still leading, to all sorts of contention, disorder, and weakness. Do you know that succeed and success are not once used in the New Testament? Why, you may ask? We are not told why, and yet the probable reason is neither obscure nor remote. Evidently the writers had no need of them, or their equivalents, in the language in which they wrote, as they had no ideas to convey at all corresponding to them, rendering their use necessary.

I claim that this is a most significant fact, and one which if properly understood and applied, would go far towards making a complete revolution in church methods and work as they exist to day. Why, sirs, is it not strange that the text book of Christianity says nothing about succeeding, or about success, and yet these words are perpetually on the lips of professing Christians, and are, indeed, the watchwords and the tests of Christian churches.

These are the common, ordinary, every day questions asked. Is he a success? Has he been a success? Is he likely to prove a success? What do you think about his chances of success? How are you getting along as a church? Are you succeeding? How have you succeeded since you adopted your new plans, and got your new minister? Has this year been a decided success in adding members to the church, in strengthening the treasury, in paying off a standing or floating debt, or in increasing the congregation? And so on, almost ad infinitum.

I am reminded of a story told of George Whitfield. The great evangelist was riding along the road, probably to fill one of his numerous preaching engagements, when he heard a voice from the ditch, that of a drunken man, call out,—"I say, Mr. Whitfield, Mr. Whitfield, you converted me." He was evidently one of Mr. Whitfield's successes, and the evangelist after quietly looking him over said, "Yes, it looks like some of my work, the Spirit of God never converted you."

It is to be feared there are a great many of these man-converted, and man-made Christians. And what produces them? A desire on the part of the minister, or the church, or both combined to make a success. The idea is that numbers make success. That if a large number of people are added to the church, and these additions are faithfully reported in the recognized denominational organ—which is almost invariably done—it will soon be taken for granted that so and so is a highly successful minister, whose services will always be at a premium, and in great demand; and that such a church is a prosperous and desirable position to occupy, and likely to be greatly sought after whenever a vacancy occurs. I am far from wishing to insinuate that these ideas are always entertained with a full consciousness of their presence and force—although I fear in many cases they are—or that all considerable ingatherings are the result of such planning and scheming; but I do contend that they are liable to be there, as an impelling force, when the one dominant idea is simply that of making a success. It is thus that poor samples of Christians are made, who prove only a weakness and a hindrance, if not something worse. Or rather it is thus that many people are persuaded they are Christians when they are not, which is probably the most fatal injury that one well meaning man can inflict upon another. And let it evermore be borne in mind that there is no case so utterly hopeless, and so likely to entail incalculable and irremediable loss, as that of an unconverted member of a Christian church.

By influences which God alone can fully estimate, and the consequent responsibility which he alone can rightly fix, the individual is brought to believe a lie concerning himself, which as a delusion of the worst kind may go on increasing through life, and abide with him in death, and not be dissipated till he stands before the judgment throne, and hears the words from the lips of the Judge : "I never knew you ; depart from me." The possibility of such a disastrous ending, to what seems to be such a fair beginning, should, at least, make the high priests who minister at the altar of success, and the devotees who worship there, pause in their mistaken and perilous devotion and zeal.

But while it is true that succeed and success are never used in the New Testament, the word faithful is used with considerable frequency. As a matter of fact it is used over forty times, and that mainly, and almost exclusively, in regard to the servants and service of God. Take a few examples out of many : " Well done, good and faithful servant; thou hast been faithful over a few things." "Let a man so account of us, as of the ministers of Christ, and stewards of the mysteries of God. Moreover it is required in stewards that a man be found faithful." "Timotheus, who is my beloved son, and faithful in the Lord." "Tychicus, a beloved brother, and faithful minister in the Lord." "Epaphras, our dear fellow servant, who is for you a faithful minister of Christ." "He counted me faithful, putting me into the ministry" "The same commit thou to faithful men, who shall be able to teach others also." "Be thou faithful unto death, and I will give thee a crown of life."

How significant is all this! How admonitory! Will the Christian church, the world throughout, take the trouble to place these facts side by side, and look at them, and see what they mean; namely, that success is not even mentioned, but that being faithful is constantly commended, and that it is the only attribute in a servant of God to which a reward is annexed. It is really a wonder that the idea of reward for successful service did not slip in somewhere, if it had any existence in the Divine thought or plan.

But perhaps you want to know whether I am not

riding this horse a little too hard, or carrying this discriminating process a little too far? I think not. I certainly have no wish to be unfair. I only wish to get at the truth, and place it as clearly as I can before others. To show that I am thoroughly sincere and honest in this matter I will go so far as to expose the one seemingly assailable point in my argument. It is this. In the parable of the talents did not the Lord commend and reward the faithful servants for successful dealing, inasmuch as in each case the deposit had been doubled by the using? That is a fair question, and fairly put, and I will try to answer it. My answer is a direct negative. No, the Lord did not commend and reward them for successful dealing, because the reverse of that is expressly stated. He did not say, well done good and successful servant, thou hast been successful over a few things, but He did say faithful servant, and faithful over a few things. It was plainly not the success of the undertaking, although that was considerable, but the fidelity, the attention to orders and just expectations, the faithful, assiduous, and rightly directed use of the talents, which secured commendation and reward. And then it is doubtful if the success achieved appeared great in the eyes of the Master. He says,—" Thou hast been faithful over *a few things,*" not many, and presumably not great. He had evidently no idea of giving them to understand that they had achieved wonders, or been eminently successful. No, his language rightly understood, inferentially if not expressly, forbids their entertaining the idea of having accomplished a notable success at all, and pins them down to the thought that it is their fidelity that has secured his approbation and reward.

But will not all faithful service be successful? The answer to that question is two-fold, Yes, and No. Yes, if you mean will not God honor such service always, and make it accomplish his purposes. No, if you mean will it always produce such large and immediate results as bear the unmistakable stamp of what men account success.

A faithful service will always secure the Divine benediction and approval, and the results will follow; but whether they will be large or small, immediate or remote, God himself will determine. We have, strictly speaking, nothing to do with success. It is not our business. That is God's business, and God's care and responsibility, and He is certainly able to take care of His own. And whenever we interfere, or attempt to interfere, with what belongs to God, trouble and weakness, if not something worse, are likely to follow. It is certain that God does not hold his servants responsible for success, but he does hold them responsible for being faithful. Says Paul: "I have planted, Apollos watered, but God gave the increase;" and any increase there may be, however large, that is not from that source, is not worth having.

And then the exact justice of God in this arrangement is quite apparent to the thoughtful mind. Being faithful is a personal quality, and is in the keeping and under the control of the individual, and he can rightly and justly be made accountable for it; but success is not in his keeping, nor under his control.

It may be promoted, or it may be hindered, by considerations and circumstances and influences outside of himself; and it is mainly dependent, as far as the operative, moral compelling force is concerned, upon the favor and blessing of Almighty God through the Spirit. So that the servant of God cannot justly be made responsible for success, neither is he; but he can justly be made responsible for fidelity, and he is.

What then should be done in view of these important considerations? Is the church of God to go on forever following the world in its methods and standards? Must Christians always go on sacrificing quality to quantity, in the different departments of Christian work, when it is well known that God has small esteem for the latter, and rates at the highest possible value the former? Must the church go on glorifying itself instead of glorifying its Great Head? In short, is the church willing to continue its world wide operations, and regulate the same by a standard which is totally misleading and absolutely false.

I am fully aware that I am bringing a very serious indictment, and one which has a widely extended application; but I claim that my position is not only tenable, but absolutely impregnable. It cannot be successfully assailed. I have said the standard is misleading as well as false, and it is misleading because it is false. Have you not known churches, year after year, chasing the phantom of success, and with constant and unvarying disappointment? Everything and everybody in turn is supposed to be at fault, and answerable for the failure, while all the while the fault is fundamental, and not being on the surface shallow minds fail to see it. The mistake is in aiming at success at all, as that word is popularly understood. Rather aim at being faithful, and whatever of success that is worth anything, and of an enduring nature, will come, and come in God's time, which is the best time.

Given a faithful minister, a faithful church with faithful office bearers, a faithful Sabbath-school superintendent, a faithful body of teachers and other workers; and all habitually and increasingly concerned to be absolutely loyal to Jesus Christ, and the result cannot be doubtful. But whatever the result, whether large or small, immediate or remote, the reward of faithful service is sure. Success may go unrewarded, but fidelity never; for, over and above the future reward whatever that may be, it brings its own reward, as unfailingly as the operation of cause and effect, in the building up and consolidation of pure and noble character. What is needed to-day in the individual Christian, in the individual church, and in the church universal, is more character and less profession; more likeness to Christ, and less pomp and show and all sorts of vain imaginings; in short, more real Christianity, and less religion.

Some one has said that the need of the church is not so much an increase in the number of Christians as an improvement in the quality of the existing type, and I know nothing that would be so likely to bring about this desirable end as that of aiming to be faithful rather than successful.

Beware of the prevailing mania for success, for it is destructive alike of character and usefulness. It is essentially a worldly spirit. I have thought deeply upon this matter, and long, and I feel strongly, and am determined to speak plainly. Success is the rock upon which the church of the nineteenth century has already sustained considerable damage, and upon which, if left to herself, she might become a wreck. It leads to all sorts of bitterness, and contention, and unholy rivalries, and large, useless expenditures of money. It sets minister against minister, congregation against congregation, church against church, denomination against denomination, and the whole against Christ, whose spirit is the very opposite of that manifested by his professed followers in their eager race for pre-eminence.

And then there is no sense in the thing anyhow. There is no recognized standard of success; that is, none to which you could gain anything like a unanimous consent.

Ask a hundred different people what a successful church is, and you may get a hundred different answers; certain it is you will get quite a number totally different, or in varying degrees of difference. With one it will be a church that has succeeded by questionable or unquestionable means in paying off a big debt. With another, it is in building and owning the finest church edifice in village, town, or city, whether it is paid for or not, or whether the contractor has gained a fair profit, or lost heavily by the transaction. With another, it is having the cleverest preacher, no matter what questionable means may have been resorted to in order to get him, or what injury inflicted upon a sister church, or ultimately upon himself. With another, it is in having the largest Sabbath-school, or a full church, or a splendid choir, or a rich, aristocratic congregation. With some it is in having rousing meetings, with plenty of talk and little doing; or a revival in progress with a large ingathering of souls.

You can never be certain what a man means by a successful church till you ask him to explain, and then the explanation may be anything but convincing and satisfactory. There are some people who are always quite sure about everything, because they don't know enough to make them modest, who will tell you that the only successful church is the one where additions are constantly being made to the membership. But then in spite of this oracular deliverance it must be borne in mind that there are churches, or at least people in them, who look upon a revival as a sort of calamity; and it may be, or it may not be. I am simply stating facts. I am not expressing an opinion. One thing only seems to be clear, that there is no recognized standard of success, that is, none which all would consent to accept. The fact is the church is losing, or has lost, its head over this thing.

You talk to the world about its mad race for wealth. The world might justly retort upon the church about its mad race for success. Let the phantom go! Pursue it no farther. It is a delusion and a snare. Simply be loyal to Christ, and always loyal, and leave the issues with Him. He, not you, is "mighty to save."

CHAPTER V.

Prayer.

THERE can be no doubt about the importance of prayer, and the pre-eminent position it occupies in the Christian system. Many and varied definitions have been given of it, but one should suffice, namely, that it is speaking with, or talking to God. Whatever else it may be, it must be that, if it be a reality at all. And herein, at the outset, we are confronted by the main difficulty regarding prayer, philosophically considered. Some one has said that a personal God is unthinkable, and there should be no difficulty, and no hesitancy, in making the admission. The fact is that all personalities, outside of our own, are unthinkable, and even that would be unthinkable apart from actual consciousness and experience. The personality of an angel is unthinkable, and so is that of a disembodied spirit, apart from contact and observation, which the many do not, as yet, deem possible.

So there need be no difficulty in admitting that such an immense personality as God, is to us, unthinkable, for it is only another way of saying that He is incomprehensible. He is so necessarily, and there the matter must rest.

We cannot, however, help, constituted as we are, associating with a person, or personality, the ideas of substance, dimension, form, and shape. And yet God has neither, as far as we can conceive, or understand. Hence, "No man hath seen God at any time." Not only has God no form, as we understand that term, but He has no history ; because a history presumes a beginning and an end, and God has neither. So that every time we attempt to touch God, feel after Him, we are met by the insoluble, and get into the region of the incomprehensible and intangible. But while we cannot think of a person without the idea of substance, of some kind, and dimension and form ; we yet have to admit the personality of God, if we admit it at all, without these things, and that necessarily.

Why necessarily? Because the moment you have

circumscribed God in your thought, if such a thing were possible, you have destroyed the fundamental idea of His being, namely, His illimitableness. "Canst thou by searching find out God; canst thou find out the Almighty unto perfection?" God is necessarily diffusive, because if He is anywhere He is everywhere. And yet we feel the necessity of localizing Him, and there is only one way in which we can do it, and that is by realizing that He is in us, and over us, and underneath us, and all about us. In other words, that because He is illimitable, He is near us, and can never be away from us, nor we away from Him. This seems to be the Psalmist's idea. "O Lord, thou hast searched me, and known me. Thou knowest my downsitting and mine uprising, thou understandest my thought afar off. Thou compassest my path and my lying down, and art acquainted with all my ways. For there is not a word in my tongue, but, lo, O Lord, thou knowest it altogether. Thou hast beset me behind and before, and laid thine hand upon me. Such knowledge is too wonderful for me; it is high, I cannot attain unto it. Whither shall I go from thy spirit? or whither shall I flee from thy presence? If I ascend up into heaven, thou art there;

if I make my bed in hell, behold, thou art there. If I take the wings of the morning, and dwell in the uttermost parts of the sea; even there shall thy hand lead me, and thy right hand shall uphold me." Psalm 139 1-10 vs.

God surrounds and permeates us as the atmosphere does. He is in us, and around us, and in a constant state of circulation through us. "In Him we live, and move, and have our being." Wherever we go He is, because He is everywhere, and we cannot flee from His presence.

Although God cannot be local, in the sense of definable limits in His person, He can be vocal, and whenever and wherever that occurs localization is practically secured; and for the time being, at least, it is actual. But this is God's act, not ours.

God was vocal to Adam and Eve in the garden. "And they heard the voice of the Lord God walking in the garden in the cool of the day. And the Lord God called unto Adam, and said unto him, Where art thou? And he said, I heard thy voice in the garden, and I was afraid. And the Lord God said unto the woman, What is this thou hast done? And the woman said, the serpent beguiled me, and I did eat."

God held converse with Cain. "And the Lord said unto Cain, why art thou wroth, and why is thy countenance fallen? And the Lord said unto Cain, where is Abel, thy brother? And he said I know not. Am I my brother's keeper. . . . And Cain said unto the Lord, my punishment is greater than I can bear."

God spake often to Noah. "And God said unto Noah, the end of all flesh is come before me; for the earth is filled with violence through them, and behold I will destroy them with the earth." He further instructed him to build the ark, giving him the exact details, and what to do when built.

And after the subsidence of the flood he spoke to him again. "And God spake unto Noah, saying go forth out of the ark, thou and thy wife, and thy sons, and thy sons' wives with thee."

God talked with Abraham, and the effect showed how real it was. "And when Abram was ninety years old and nine, the Lord appeared to Abram, and said unto him, I am the Almighty God; walk before Me, and be thou perfect, and I will make my covenant between Me and thee, and will multiply thee exceedingly. And Abram fell on his face, and God talked with him saying: As for Me, behold, my covenant is with thee, and thou shalt be a father of many nations. Neither shalt thy name any more be called Abram, but thy name shalt be Abraham, for a father of many nations have I made thee." Gen. 17 ch., 1-5 vs.

God spake many times unto Moses, the most remarkable being that on the Mount, at the giving of the law. "And Moses went up unto God, and the Lord called unto him out of the mountain. And the Lord said unto Moses: Lo, I come unto thee in a thick cloud, that the people may hear when I speak with thee, and believe thee forever. And when the voice of the trumpet sounded long, and waxed louder and louder, Moses spake, and God answered him *by a voice*. And the Lord came down upon Mount Sinai, on the top of the Mount; and the Lord called Moses up to the top of the Mount, and Moses went up. And all the people saw the thunderings and the lightnings, and the noise of the trumpet and the mountain smoking; and when the people saw it, they removed, and stood afar off. And Moses drew near unto the thick darkness where God was. And the Lord said unto Moses, thus thou shalt say unto the children of Israel, ye have seen that I have talked with you from heaven." Ex. 19-20 chs.

I am quite willing to admit that the personality of God cannot be demonstrated by human reason; that it is, in fact, incomprehensible to the human mind, and that therefore those who depend upon reason alone may be expected to find insuperable difficulties strewing their path in their march Godward, if they mean to move in that direction at all.

But it is plain from the instances quoted, and others that might be, that notwithstanding His illimitableness God has, and God can, localize and vocalize Himself, in such a way as to give a satisfying conception of His personality, to those who are willing to accept His word and be instructed by it.

I find no fault with those who reject the Bible as an inspired book, if they fail to entertain the personality of God as a personal belief, and fall back upon the theory that what we call God is simply a great controlling and upholding force. Although they might, perhaps, be pushed so as to make them admit that the force they perceive and believe in is an intelligent one, and therefore, possibly, at least, resident in a personality. I say they might be pushed thus far, and logically so too; but they cannot be pushed far enough to admit the personality as demonstrable from their standpoint; that is from the standpoint of pure reason, because it is simply incomprehensible.

But for those who accept the Bible as a guide there is no excuse, for that supplements our reason, and helps us to a conception and knowledge that we could not otherwise attain unto.

Reason then, in a certain measure, aids us in our search after God, but it cannot enable us to apprehend His personality. The Bible does that for us, for therein it is revealed that God can localize himself when necessary, and speak with a voice and in language that we can understand But some may contend that these conversations are imaginary. The true believer in the Bible will not think so. To give up their literality and reality would be giving away all that they are worth to us, for they establish the personality, a thing so necessary in approaching God. Hence, "he that cometh to God must believe that He is": that is, great and mighty as He unquestionably is, and incomprehensible to us, He is yet a person whom we can approach, and to whom we can speak.

What is the proper habitude, or frame of mind, in

which we should approach God? The general and popular belief is that it should be one of awe and deep solemnity. I am disposed to question the correctness of that belief; and I don't mean by that, that we are to run to the other extreme, and be frivolous—far from that. I mean that when we approach God, in prayer, we are not coming into the presence of the King, or before the Judge, but we are approaching "Our Father which art in heaven," and the spirit suitable for that is neither fear nor solemn awe, but filial feeling and child-like trust.

God is represented as pitying us in the same way that an earthly father pities his children, but with the additional advantage of having a perfect knowledge of what we are, by which his compassion can be made more available. The pity of an earthly parent for his child, far and constantly, outruns his opportunities and his knowledge. If he knew more he would do more, and gladly and freely too; but his always limited power is still further limited by the necessary limitations of his knowledge.

Here God has the advantage, and His pity the larger scope for its exercise, "for he knoweth our frame, he remembereth that we are dust." He knows what we are, our formation, our make-up, our surroundings, our weaknesses, our temptations, our exact power of resistance at all times, and the nature and strength of the tempting power He can effectively pity, and effectively help, because He knows all. And He never forgets. " He remembereth that we are dust." He keeps that in mind all the time. So that when we put all these things together, what we are necessitated, by nature and experience, to understand by the term father : what we know God must be when we approach Him in that capacity, and not in the capacity of a king or a judge ; and what the Word states as to His perfect knowledge of us, and His abiding tenderness and love towards us : when we sum up all these things, we at once see that in coming before Him it should not be in fear and awe, but with simple, childlike confidence that knows no fear, and even with some amount of that legitimate familiarity which genuine confidence always engenders.

Yes, I say, familiarity, but I am far from meaning irreverence, or anything like that, or even approaching to it. I mean, in fact, the very opposite ; a familiarity that springs from confidence, sincerity and love ; and with this God is always well pleased.

One of the most remarkable examples we have of this child-like familiarity with God in prayer, is that of the eminent and good man who has passed to his reward, Charles Haddon Spurgeon. Remarkable as he was as a preacher, compelling the rapt attention of thousands by the witchery of his magnificent voice, his plain language, his homely illustrations, his seraphic fervor, and his Pauline zeal, he was still more remarkable in prayer. In that he was earnest, simple, and familiar. Whether in the home, by the sick bed, in the prayer meeting, or in the vast congregation, he literally talked with God in the simplest and the most familiar forms of utterance. Some people thought he was flippant, and irreverent; greatly lacking in solemnity, and not sufficiently conscious of the greatness and majesty of God.

But he knew more of God than his critics, and what seemed to them undue familiarity was really the result of a more vivid conception of God as a real personality, and a closer and deeper acquaintance with Him as a loving Father, than is ordinarily possessed. No one ever seemed to doubt that he was talking to God when he was praying.

With many ministers it is, unfortunately, the reverse;

that is, you are frequently in considerable doubt whether they are talking to God or the congregation. What does all this mean about flying off in prayer, in fine rhetorical language, about the greatness, the majesty, and the glory of God? It is out of place. God doesn't need it. God doesn't want it. We are not required to approach Him as a great and august personage, inspiring feelings of awe and deep solemnity, but as a Father who loves us, and pities us, and cares for us, and who is pleased to hold simple, familiar converse with His children. Christ settled that point, for ever, when he said, "After this manner therefore pray ye, Our Father which art in heaven."

And it is worthy of remark that Christ is perfectly consistent with Himself, and invariably tells us to make our approaches to God as a Father, and to think of Him, and resort to Him constantly in that capacity. "Pray to thy Father which is in secret, and thy Father which seeth in secret shall reward thee openly." "Your Father knoweth what things ye have need of before ye ask him." "If ye then, being evil, know how to give good gifts unto your children, how much more shall your Father which is in heaven give good things to them that ask him." "If two of you shall agree on earth as touching anything that they shall ask, it shall be done for them of my Father which is in heaven." "When ye stand praying, forgive, if ye have aught against any, that your Father also, which is in heaven, may forgive you your trespasses. But if ye do not forgive, neither will your Father wich is in heaven forgive your trespasses." "The hour cometh, and now is, when the true worshippers shall worship the Father in spirit and in truth, for the Father seeketh such to worship Him." "Whatsoever ye shall ask the Father in my name, he will give it you." "The Father himself loveth you, because ye have loved me, and have believed that I came out from God."

We have also Christ's example to guide us in this matter. He is not only consistent with Himself, but He is also consistent with His own teaching. What He taught His disciples to do He did Himself. His invariable habit was to address God as Father. There is only one exception, as far as I can find out, and that was in that supreme moment of His great agony upon the cross, when He felt He had lost His Father, and He " cried with a loud voice, saying, Eli, Eli, lama sabachthani; that is to say, My God, My God, why hast thou forsaken me."

As examples of the invariableness of His practice of addressing God as Father take the following: " I thank thee, O Father, Lord of heaven and earth, because thou hast hid these things from the wise and prudent, and hast revealed them unto babes. " Even so, Father, for so it seemed good in thy sight." " Jesus lifted up his eyes, and said, Father, I thank thee that thou hast heard me; and I know that thou hearest me always." " These words spake Jesus, and lifted up his eyes to heaven, and said Father, the hour is come." " Now is my soul troubled, and what shall I say? Father save me from this hour; but for this cause came I unto this hour. Father, glorify thy name." " O my Father, if it be possible, let this cup pass from me; nevertheless, not as I will, but as Thou wilt. " He went away again the second time, and prayed, saying, O my Father, if this cup may not pass away from me, except I drink it, Thy will be done." " Then said Jesus, Father forgive them, for they know not what they do." " When Jesus had cried with a loud voice, he said, Father into thy hands I commend my spirit; and having said this he gave up the ghost."

So our contention should not be difficult of admission, and if admitted and acted upon it is beyond all price, namely, that in making our approaches to God, in prayer, we come to Him in no other capacity than that of a child to a father, and with sentiments of pure and entire affection, and complete confidence. We do not fear, we love; for love hath cast out fear.

Having settled, I hope with some measure of clearness and satisfaction, the personality of God, and the spirit in which we should approach Him, there remains for consideration the question as to what we are justified in expecting from Him.

We are confronted with a serious difficulty at the outset, which probably will go far towards explaining many of our disappointments in prayer. It is this: God's estimate of the material and the spiritual, the temporal and the eternal, is diffierent, very different, from ours; or rather, our estimate is, unfortunately, not the same as His. His estimate of the spiritual and the eternal is large, and of the material and temporal small; that is, relatively so, at least.

We, such is our nature and the force of circumstances, have a constant tendency to reverse that order. Hence we are liable, and constantly liable, to ask for what He is least disposed to grant, and not to ask for what He is most disposed to give. Or, to put the same idea in a somewhat different form, our estimate of what is needed for our real well-being, is apt to be different to God's, hence disappointment, not uncommonly, ensues.

And this, unfortunately, must evermore be so, so long as God is what He is, and we are what we are; or until we recognize the conditions, and give up everything to Him; for He can see all the way, but we cannot see, in advance, a single step of the journey.

From this it is not necessary for us to think that God is unmindful of our temporal well-being for we know He is not. He simply forms a more correct estimate than we do, and therein is the sole difference. He gave us this life, and He expects us to do the best we can with it. Food and raiment, and other temporal things, are necessary for the sustenance, and comfort, and perpetuation of life; and these are promised in conjunction with our honest efforts to obtain and to enjoy. But they are only means to an end, not the end itself, and that end is spiritual and eternal.

But are we justified in expecting God to give us what

we ask for, or may we expect Him to grant our requests, without fail, when they are made known to Him?

Some people say we are, and that their experience justifies the expectation. I have always felt somewhat at a loss to know what to say to these good people, for I cannot admit their contention, at least as a principle generally applicable, and I do not like to call in question their veracity. I simply content myself by saying that I think they are mistaken, or if not mistaken, that their experience is not the average; and if they put it forth as the average, as what all may expect, they are liable to inflict considerable discouragement and damage upon those whose experience is not, by a long way, so favorable as theirs. I think the average experience is that good people ask a great many things of God that are not granted. Besides it may be as well to bear in mind that it is in the very nature of a petition, whether presented to God or anybody else, that it may be denied; because if it may not be denied it ceases to be a petition, and really assumes the authority and dimensions of a command.

But my extremely fortunate and greatly favored friend and brother, will probably say in reply to this, that he does not say that a petition may not be denied, but that it will not be. Well, that is merely cavilling about words, for experience testifies that what may be, in a certain proportion of cases will be.

But what about those definite promises in regard to prayer, by which, if language means anything, we are led most certainly to expect that we shall receive what we ask for? Let us look at some of them. "Ask and it shall be given you, seek and ye shall find, knock and it shall be opened unto you. For every one that asketh receiveth, and he that seeketh findeth, and to him that knocketh it shall be opened." "If two of you shall agree on earth as touching anything that they shall ask, it shall be done for them of my Father which is in heaven." "All things, whatsoever ye shall ask in prayer, believing, ye shall receive." "What things soever ye desire, when ye pray, believe that ye receive them, and ye shall have them." "Whatsoever ye shall ask in my name, that will I do, that the Father may be glorified in the Son. If ye shall ask anything in my name I will do it." "Whatsoever ye shall ask the Father in my name, He will give it you." "If ye abide in me, and my words abide in you, ye shall ask what ye will, and it shall be done unto you." "Whatsoever we ask, we receive of Him, because we keep His commandments, and do those things that are pleasing in His sight." "This is the confidence that we have in Him, that, if we ask any thing according to his will, he heareth us."

It will be observed that the first promise here quoted is absolutely unconditional, and it comes from the lips of Christ, whence all the others proceed, except the last two. We are told, in the plainest way, to ask, and seek, and knock; and we shall receive, and find, and the door will be opened. Then as if to make it more emphatic, and absolute, and place it beyond all doubt and controversy, the universality and unfailing nature of the experience is affirmed, "for everyone that asketh receiveth, and he that seeketh findeth, and to him that knocketh it shall be opened."

The second promise has a definite condition attached, namely, harmony or agreement; "if two of you shall agree," etc. The third and fourth have faith annexed to them as a condition; "believing, ye shall receive; believe that ye receive them," etc. The fifth and sixth are based upon the condition of asking in Christ's name; "if ye shall ask anything in my name"; "whatsoever ye shall ask the Father in my name," etc. The seventh has the condition attached of our abiding in Christ, and His words abiding in us; "if ye abide in me and my words abide in you," etc. The eighth is based upon obedience; "we receive of him, because we keep his commandments," etc. The last is based upon conformity to God's will; "if we ask anything according to his will he heareth us."

Now there cannot be any difficulty about the last statement, because it is self-evident that God certainly will both hear and answer any and all prayers that are according to His will. He must do so, in fact, to be consistent with Himself, and He cannot be inconsistent. With Him, to will is to do. The two things are simultaneous and identical in Him, but not in us. In us they are different and separate, though closely connected, but in Him they are the same. Therefore there can be no failure in anything that is in harmony with His will. Prayers that fulfil that condition must be answered. There can be no may-be about it, if prayers are answered at all.

But have we any satisfactory and convincing means of deciding when our prayers are in harmony with the

Divine will? That, from surface considerations, may seem an easy question to answer, but if you will go deeper you will be liable to think it is not so easy. Take this case, for instance, as an illustration: We know, certainly, that God must, and God does desire the salvation of men. We know it because we have His word for it, given with a most peculiar and exceptional emphasis. God stakes the reality of His existence, as a solemn pledge, of his absolute sincerity in this respect. "As I live, saith the Lord God, I have no pleasure in the death of the wicked, but that the wicked turn from his way and live."

We would naturally conclude from this, that prayer offered for the conversion of some one in whom we have a deep interest, would be in harmony with the Divine will, and that it would most certainly be answered. But such a conclusion, while it may follow, does not necessarily follow, and for this reason: We must take into account the free agency of man. God cannot save a man in spite of himself, or against his will. Man is a responsible, consenting party to his salvation, and without that consent, freely given, he cannot be saved. Nothing is clearer than this, from the nature of man as a moral agent, and from the explict statements of Scripture regarding it. And from this the conclusion is irresistible—startling as the statement may appear—that God is not likely to have willed the salvation of a man who obstinately and persistently wills his own condemnation.

That is one side of the question. There is another side equally truthful, and much more comforting for many an anxious soul. It is this: That while God will not do violence to man's moral nature, even to save him, He can, such are His infinite resources, constrain him to freely and gladly accept, what, if left to himself, he might reject. And we have the statement of Christ that God does exercise this peculiar power, this sweet and sacred violence, to draw men to Himself. "No man can come to Me, except the Father which hath sent Me draw him, and I will raise him up at the last day." So that looking at the matter, in all its bearings, it would seem that we are justified in coming to the conclusion, that prayer offered for the salvation of others, is in harmony with the Divine will and a favorable response may be confidently expected.

But by far the most serious difficulty in regard to

prayer arises in connection with the promise which is absolutely unconditional,—"Ask and it shall be given you, seek and ye shall find, knock and it shall be opened unto you. For every one that asketh receiveth, and he that seeketh findeth, and to him that knocketh it shall be opened."

How to harmonize the average Christian experience with that promise and that statement seems impossible. And we shall not get rid of the difficulty by shutting our eyes to it, and affecting to ignore it. Better look at it, fairly and squarely, and if possible stare it out of countenance, and out of existence.

It will not, however, meet the difficulty to say that a condition is implied, which is quite a favorite way some people have of getting over these rough places. There are two fatal objections to such a supposition. The first is, that it is a very unsafe law of interpretation, and capable, when admitted, of being greatly abused. The second is, that it is extremely unlikely that Christ intended a condition to be implied, because he was certainly in the habit of stating conditions when He deemed them necessary to guard, and at the same time, fully express His meaning. It was his almost invariable custom to supply a condition, as we see by the quotations given, and the present one seems to be the solitary exception to the rule. No, it is not reasonable to suppose that a condition is implied. That will not get us over the difficulty. What then ?

Some people will tell you that it can be met by saying that God sometimes answers prayer by not answering it. All that is necessary to say about that is, that it is as absolutely absurd and self-contradictory a statement as any man, in or out of his senses, could make. And yet it has been made, many a time, in all seriousness, and accepted without question as a very sagacious observation, and a profound truth. What Shakespeare says, in his "Antony and Cleopatra," regarding prayer, may have had something to do with the origin and currency of this idea about a denial being, in some mysterious manner, an answer.

> "We ignorant of ourselves,
> Beg often our own harms, which the wise powers
> Deny us for our good; so find we profit,
> By losing of our prayers."

Here it is frankly admitted that we may lose our prayers ; that is, they may not be granted ; and yet, in certain circumstances, we may gain a negative good by the refusal, which is simply the absence of a positive evil.

We miss the possible evil by not receiving the answer. And here it may be worthy of observation that Shakespeare, in this instance, fails somewhat in his usual fine discrimination of thonght, and exactness of expression. Profit means, and always means, something gained and added to our present possessions ; and a negative good, or exemption from possible positive evil, cannot be said to be an addition to what already exists. The fact is, that no amount of sophistry, however clever, and neither Shakespeare nor anybody else, can make a negative a positive,—not while the world stands.

Then, again, we are told by some grave commentators, and some easy going preachers, that of course God may not give us just exactly what we ask for, but He, nevertheless, answers our prayers by giving us something different. and perhaps just as good, or better. It ought to be sufficient to say, in answer to this, that such an explanation of a grave difficulty is an absolute denial of common sense ; and whenever you divorce Christianity, or any part of it, from common sense, you simply succeed in making it ridiculous.

Besides, just look at what immediately follows the

unconditional promise we are considering, "Or what man is there of you, whom if his son ask bread, will he give him a stone? or if he ask a fish will he give him a serpent? If ye then, being evil, know how to give good gifts unto your children, how much more shall your Father which is in heaven give good things to them that ask him?" No, Sir, the reception of something other than what is asked for is not an answer to prayer, and all the clever sophists in the church cannot persuade me that it is. And allow me also to add, that if you are offering such explanations to God's discouraged and afflicted children, you are giving them a stone instead of bread, and a serpent instead of a fish. Such expositions of the Divine intentions and promises are unsatisfactory, misleading, useless, derogatory to God, and an unspeakable bitterness and disappointment to His people, in the times of their greatest need. It is like feeding a hungry man on the Apples of Sodom : nothing but ashes are left in the mouth, and a bitter taste.

O, it is sad, unutterably sad, pitiable in the extreme, enough to make an angel weep, and the Christ of God to shed tears again, to see the wretched, miserable attempts that are sometimes made, by shallow, well-meaning people, to give comfort to a soul stricken with a great and enduring sorrow. Relying upon a definite promise of answer to prayer he has asked, as a child would ask, for a great good, and to his unspeakable astonishment and dismay he has received what he cannot but regard as a great evil. And you tell him, poor miserable comforter as you are, that a condition was implied, though not expressed; or that God has really and truly answered by denying his request; or that He has given him something else instead, which may turn out to be a great good; and you expect him to be comforted, but alas, he is not. Then you tell him he is rebellious, but he shakes his head, and with a look that should make your heart ache, quietly throws back your ungenerous imputation.

He is simply dazed, confused, confounded. He does not know what to make of it all. He can see no harmony between the promise upon which he relied, and which caused him to hope, and his experience; and your explanations do not help him to surmount the difficulty. Can anything be done for him? Yes, if you know what, and how. Take him by the hand, and look kindly into his face, and in soft but firm tones tell him that that Being to whom he prayed, and upon whose promise he relied, is a Soverign, and that He can do what he likes with His own; and that therefore His right to give or withhold cannot be called in question. Tell him that Divine Sovereignty is antecedent to Revelation; that it was an essential and fundamental part of God, a whole eternity of years, before a single line of the Bible was written, or any promise was ever made to man; and that nothing the Bible contains can alter that, or ever was intended to alter it. Tell him, too, that when God talks with His children He has to use such language as they can understand to show His willingness to hear, to answer, and to help; but He cannot abdicate His sovereign right to be the supreme judge of what is best in any given circumstances.

Christ Himself recognized this, when, in dark Gethsemane, He said, "O my Father, if it be possible, let this cup pass from me; nevertheless not as I will, but as Thou wilt." And then again, "O my Father, if this cup may not pass away from me, except I drink it, Thy will be done."

That solves the difficulty, and nothing else will; for

He who was the mouthpiece of the Father, in bidding us hope, when He said, "Ask and it shall be given you, seek and ye shall find, knock and it shall be opened unto you," Himself recognized the necessary limitation imposed by the Divine Sovereignty. "Thy will be done," is the sum of it all. Only prayers in harmony with the Divine will can be answered. "And this is the confidence that we have in him, that, if we ask anything according to His will He heareth us. And if we know that He heareth us, whatsoever we ask, we know that we have the petitions that we desired of Him." 1 John 5 ch. 14-15 vs.

CHAPTER VI.

The Prayer Meeting.

THE prayer meeting is a time-honored and all but universal institution in the Christian church. Could it be attended and conducted as it unquestionably should be, it might become the most potent agency for good, and the most profitable of all the means of grace. And yet the general experience is far, very far, from realizing this possibility, or this ideal as some people might choose to call it. I have attended prayer meetings at different times, in different places, with different denominations of Christians, extending over quite a considerable number of years ; and simple honesty compels me to make the sad and melancholy confession, that with only a solitary exception here and there could any individual meeting be called, by any stretch of charity, anything but a weekly formality. As a rule, with a few notable exceptions, I have found the attendance small and the exercises of the most formal character.

It may be that my experience has been unfortunate and exceptional. Upon that I am not prepared to express an opinion. I give it honestly for what it is worth, and I have a strong suspicion that many others, if equally honest, could confirm it.

I have it on unquestioned authority that in a certain influential and aristocratic church in one of our chief cities, which has a large membership and a still larger congregation, and pays its eloquent young minister about three thousand dollars a year, there were present recently, at the usual weekly prayer meeting, nine persons all told, perhaps the minister made the tenth. Evidently the weekly meeting for prayer is not esteemed very highly in that congregation.

There are, as we know, different methods of conducting a prayer meeting. First, there is what may be called the regular service method. In this the minister, or leader, assumes the whole responsibility and work of the meeting, and it differs from the ordinary service on the Lord's day only in its being not quite so elaborate nor so lengthy. It is strictly speaking a religious service, and it is altogether a misnomer to call it a prayer meeting. It is a week-night service, and nothing more nor less.

Another method is that of calling upon brethren to pray, leaving nothing to voluntariness or spontaneity. The plea for this method generally is, that few or none will respond unless the call is made.

There are two well founded objections to this method. The first is, that generally a certain number of brethren who are supposed to be—whether they are or not—both willing and able to engage in prayer, with propriety and profit, are called upon constantly, and a monotony is engendered which is felt to be anything but delightful, and is certainly anything but profitable. A rut is made, and ruts are proverbially difficult to get out of.

The second objection is that it is a temporary violation of human freedom in one of the most, if not the most, important and sacred engagements of a man's life. Nothing, when properly understood, can possibly be more important or more sacred than that of prayer, whether in private or in public; and whatever of compulsion or force is brought to bear on that is clearly wrong. But you say there is no force when a man is called upon in meeting to engage in prayer. I know there is not, and yet I know there is, and you know it too; and you know also that there is no essential contradiction in this statement, although it may look like one.

It is not necessary to explain or illustrate this matter further to any one who knows experimentally what is meant, and to any one who does not, scarcely any amount of explanation or illustration would suffice to make it perfectly clear. It is really and practically a violation of human freedom, although it is not meant as such; and no one should, at any time, be called upon to pray in public, unless his consent has been previously obtained I will, even, go further than this, and say that no man should pray unless he has an earnest desire, and a God-inspired impulse in that direction, to present a definite petition to the Almighty for himself or for others.

But you say a Christian should be ready at all times to pray. I am not so sure of that as you are, or seem to be, but I am sure of this—as a matter of fact which I think no one can successfully dispute—that the average

Christian is not always in a praying mood ; and I am also sure that one should not be a hypocrite in this important and sacred exercise, neither should he allow himself to be made one to suit anybody's will or convenience. Prayer is like a good deal of our modern Christianity ; we should aim more at improving the quality than increasing the quantity. Pray less and pray better would not be a bad motto to adopt and follow.

While upon this part of the subject I may as well take the opportunity of adverting to a thought which has been a long time in my mind, waiting for a fitting and favorable opportunity to express. It is in regard to prayer by the minister as a part of the public service of the sanctuary on the Lord's day. With the custom of reciting forms of prayer I am not dealing now, but with extemporaneous utterances common to several denominations of Christians which are well known, and need not be mentioned here.

The universal custom has been established, and is implicitly followed, of a minister offering never less than one, and in some cases as many as four prayers, during any single service in which he may engage. Custom has wrought the matter into an inexorable law which few, if any, seem to have courage enough to set at defiance, however much they may, in their hearts, sometimes wish to do so.

The minister, like the average Christian, is not always in a praying mood, and it would be far better for him not to pray when he feels, from whatever cause, that he has no Divine impulsion in that direction. No man should preach without that Divine impulse, much less should he attempt to address God in prayer without it. He should be accorded a wise discretion in the conduct of every service that may go to the extent of leaving out the prayer altogether, if he deem it best occasionally so to do. There would be an immense gain in many ways. A gain in reality and sincerity, very much needed. A gain in a larger acceptance with God in consequence of becoming more real and more sincere. A gain in the accession of more elasticity, a larger liberty and the breaking down of the domination of mere custom and habit. A gain in deliverance from many formal, cold, wearisome, and unprofitable prayers. The fact is that the tyranny of custom and the despotism of fashion are, in some respects, just as potent and operative in the church as they are in the world. Get rid of cumbersome machinery, and dull monotonous routine, as much as possible, and you will have a purer spirit, a larger liberty, and a fuller life.

The third method of conducting a prayer meeting which I propose to mention, and which I am disposed to endorse, is that which may be best described as the prayer and conference meeting. It has its weaknesses and imperfections, in the working, just as other methods have, but it probably meets with the largest amount of favor, and is the most extensively adopted and practised. It consists, as is well known, in about one half the time being occupied by the leader, and the balance being left to the meeting for free, voluntary, individual efforts in prayer and exhortation.

I revert to my former statement, and am prepared to justify it, that the prayer meeting might become the most potent agency for good, and the most profitable of all the means of grace. To make it this, in any individual church, or in all the churches of Christ where it has an acknowledged place, several things are required, which I will now proceed to notice.

1. The fundamental requisite is that *its paramount importance, and its vast potentiality for good* must be

generally conceded and recognized. If there are any skeptics they must be converted from their skepticism. Those who are cold, formal, and indifferent must be roused into something like interest and life. The wet blankets must, if possible, be wrung out and dried, so that they may be a comfort instead of a chill and a desolation. An enthusiasm must, by some means, be aroused in the entire community, from the minister down to the humblest member, and a firm faith engendered and established as to the utility and vast possibilities of the institution. It is too often regarded as of secondary importance, whereas it should be looked upon as of the very first importance. It is liable to be viewed as a simple necessity or duty whereby Christian character and profession may body forth some sort of formal consistency, whereas it is a privilege, and one of the highest, and the means for quickening and sustaining the life, and expressing the power of the church. It is an old saying and a true one, that the prayer meeting is the pulse of the church, that by which the sign of its life may be measured, and in which its full heart throbs, imparting life and vigor to every member of the body. It seems a two-fold purpose; when it is weak, it not only shows that the church is weak, but it further induces weakness by producing chilliness in the hearts of the few faithful ones who are struggling to uphold it. When it is strong, it is not only an evidence of the strength of the church, but it produces strength by warming, and cheering, and blessing the hearts of all.

2. *Much depends upon leadership.* A good and efficient leader is necessary to a good meeting. Those who are present will, in the main, take their cue from him, and catch his spirit. His demeanor and bearing will be infectious. To a large extent what he is, at the time, the meeting will be. If he is dull, and cold, and formal, the meeting is apt to be the same. If he is lively, earnest, devotional, enthusiastic, the meeting will feel his warmth and geniality, and respond to his earnestness, enthusiasm, and devotion. He should therefore be impressed with his responsibility, and realize, every time, how much depends upon him, and prepare and bear himself accordingly. He can make or mar the meeting. He has the first chance. He is in at the start, and as he leads others are likely to follow. He should make the best possible preparation. The hymns should all be selected beforehand, and selected with

great care and discrimination ; hymns that are familiar, and with good, lively tunes ; and they should bear, as far as practicable, upon the subject that is to be introduced, so that there will be harmony, and a completeness of effect. At the same time care should be taken not to repeat the same hymns too often, however good they may be.

The portion of scripture selected for reading should be short, and it is of the greatest importance that it should be well read, with that just and discriminating emphasis which is the best commentary. The prayer also should possess the same characteristics. The exposition, or exhortation, should be short and very definite. The aim should be to have one clearly defined thought, not many. If there are many, people get bewildered, and they end in catching on to nothing. But one thought clearly defined, explained, illustrated, and driven home, will fix itself in every mind, and produce a unity and permanency of impression, and a quickening and fructifying effect. When people are plainly and clearly instructed, and get fairly roused by the earnest thought of another, they require no prompting to either speak or pray.

3. *Due preparation of heart is required.* There is something to be done before you enter the house of prayer, if you would have and enjoy God's blessing when you get there. It is safe to say that this is very much neglected. Indeed, we might ask whether, in the majority of cases, it is so much as thought of as a necessity at all. Thought and care are given to other matters of less importance. Due preparation is invariably made as far as the adornment of the person is concerned. Time is always found for the putting on of a suitable garb to appear respectable before men, while, perhaps, the heart is left entirely unprepared. It is the soul and not the body that is to be blessed, the inner man and not the outer, and therefore that should have all needed preparation for the blessing. Wherever and whenever it is practicable let some time be spent in silent meditation and prayer before you go to the meeting, and your profit will be larger, and more manifest to yourselves and to others.

4. *Punctuality is an essential element,* therefore be punctual, and always so, as far as possible. Punctuality is a habit, and so is unpunctuality, and one of the worst kind, engendering all sorts of discomfort and disorder.

One is to be cultivated, and it is worth cultivation ; the other is to be shunned as you would shun the devil. The unpunctual attendant is apt to carry along with him a feeling of worry and confusion, that not only interferes with his own comfort and spiritual well being, but is apt, by sheer contagion, to spread to other people, and thus anything but a feeling of calmness and devotion is engendered. Let not a few but all be there at the time announced. It is easier, and certainly much pleasanter, to be punctual than to be unpunctual when the habit is once formed. It is true the best and most methodical of people may, by stress of circumstances, be behind occasionally. It is not occasional but habitual unpunctuality that is so injurious and reprehensible. There are some good people who make it a rule not to leave their homes until the time for commencing the meeting; hence they succeed, admirably, in being very punctual, or at least regular, in their unpunctuality. It is a bad habit which those who are the subjects of should try to get rid of as soon as possible. A meeting may end with a full attendance, but if it is to be really and truly profitable it should have a good beginning, and one way of securing this is by commencing with a full attendance.

It engenders warmth of heart, and it is well to be warm to begin with.

The leader should be punctual, too, not only in being there in good time, but also in commencing the meeting and ending it. Commence on time, and leave off on time, to the minute, if possible. It is setting a good example, and it is being just to those who are present. If you prolong a meeting beyond the time which it is generally understood it should occupy—an hour at the most—and especially if it be somewhat frequently repeated, some, and perhaps many, may take it as as an injustice, and quietly resent it by staying away.

5. *There should be union of spirit and of purpose, aud, as far as practicable, of sentiment.* Much depends upon this. Christ said: "If two of you shall agree on earth as touching anything that they shall ask, it shall be done for them of my Father which is in heaven." We read also in the Acts of the Apostles that "They all were with one accord in one place." Now, while it is true that all prayers are necessarily subject to the Divine Sovereignty, and will be answered or denied as God sees to be wisest and best, it is also true that when certain specified conditions are complied with, the probability of a favorable

response is increased. Unanimity, agreement, harmony, are essential elements in a profitable meeting. . The sad weakness is that Christians are seldom sufficiently agreed " as touching anything that they shall ask." Indeed, I fear the rule is that there is no accordance, nothing definite, nothing agreed upon, no conveying the united desire upon one specific matter, and calling upon God unitedly in prayer for that.

There are exceptions it is true, rare exceptions, but the exceptions, in this as in other cases, prove the rule to be what is here stated. We should aim at converting the exception into the rule, and if we succeed, even in a measure, the blessed results will soon be seen.

6. *Closeness of association and contact is necessary as a contributary effect.* People who really love one another, and are glad to see one another, do not, as a rule, exemplify their attachment by sitting a dozen yards apart, if there is any fair chance of approaching nearer, without offending the recognized proprieties; and, happily, there is that chance in a prayer meeting. And yet it is strange how isolated and repellant some people are when they ought to be, by their very profession, something altogether different. There are brethren, in

every church, who always develop a peculiar penchant for sitting very near the door, and there can be no wonder if they feel very cold, especially when the mercury has taken the hospitable fit of going below zero.

In a small meeting sometimes, especially if it be in a large room, the brethren and sisters, who profess to love one another so much, sit so far apart that it becomes necessary to speak of them as occupying different geographical positions; some north, a few south, one or two east, and some lonely brother west. This should not be. It is injurious. Whether few or many it is better to keep close together. It shows the reality of brotherly and sisterly feeling.

Besides, apart from that, there is something in magnetism. By close proximity we are likely to influence one another for good more powerfully. We give and we receive. If you want to make a fire you must not only have plenty of wood, but you must put each piece in some measure of contact with another. You may burn all the wood in the country, but you will never get the kind of fire you want, or that will be of any practical use, by lighting and burning each piece separately. So it is in a prayer meeting. Each individual may have, in some degree, the elements of spiritual light and warmth, but you cannot make a fire, which will diffuse its genial and comforting and quickening influences through all, unless you get all together, in the closest contact, actually, sympathetically, and spiritually. The larger the number the greater the probability of interest, mutual edification, and profit. A large meeting is generally more interesting than a small one. It is a law of nature as well as of grace, or rather the same law runs through both.

7. *As soon as the meeting is left open there should be an instant response,* and a thorough and general communication of thought and sympathy, in testimony and prayer; and I am inclined to add that this will, generally, be the case when the leadership is what it should be. It cannot be too much emphasized that much, very much, depends upon efficient leadership. Secure that and the rest will follow. Each one should feel it his duty and privilege to contribute his share to the general interest. Each should feel that the profitableness of the meeting is in some measure dependent upon him.

Each should realize a share of responsibility. It

is a grave mistake, but withal a prevalent one, to leave the couduct of the meeting to a stereotyped few, however excellent they may be. There is some spiritual force in every brother if he likes to let it out, and it should come out for the general benefit. We come to such meetings to minister as well as to be ministered unto. Cast out the devil. He is always intruding himself. I verily believe he is more busy there than anywhere. If, as the hymn informs us he "trembles when he sees the weakest saint upon his knees," we may imagine his concern when he sees a number of saints gathered together expressly for prayer. He will certainly not fail to do all he can to hinder. He will prevent you joining in the exercises if he possibly can. He will tell you that you are not able to speak or pray with any credit to yourself or profit to others. Pay no heed to his insinuations. Sternly refuse to be influenced by him. Tell him he is a liar from the beginning, and the father of lies. "Resist the devil and he will flee from you." "Whom resist steadfast in the faith."

If you are prompted, from within, to say a few words or pray, rise upon your feet at the first opportunity and do it, and don't let the devil dissuade you by any of his specious suggestions or arguments. In seeking to bless others you will be all the more blessed yourself; for no one gets such profit out of a meeting as he who takes some voluntary part, however humble. And be not discouraged by your seeming failures. You may not on every occasion, succeed to your own satisfaction, but take comfort and encouragement from the thought that if you are really sincere, God may make His strength manifest in your weakness, and may convey, through your faltering words, a blessing to some one.

One mistake is very common, and it acts as a discouragement, especially to beginners, in this kind of service. They are apt to think that people who speak and pray often, and are thereby familiarized with the exercise, do it with perfect self composure, and with little or no difficulty, while they are always in a tremble and a fright.

Consequently they are apt to think they are fully justified in leaving the speaking and praying mostly with the old hands, the veterans in the service. Believe me, the whole thing is a mistake, and arises from an entire misconception of the facts. Take the testimony of one who knows, and who has at least the reputation of being able to speak off hand, without the slightest apparent diffidence or difficulty, that the most experienced and the readiest speaker never entirely overcomes a natural reluctance to rise on his feet, for the purpose of saying even, a few words, to any audience, whether it be large or small; and others equally experienced, and perhaps more so, will readily confirm the absolute truthfulness of this statement. No, you must never expect to conquer entirely that peculiar besetment of all speakers, a natural diffidence and tremor at the start. It may decrease, in a measure, by practice, but it probably will never wholly disappear, and you need not expect it.

If you want to speak with a fair measure of comfort to yourself, and profit to others, you must closely observe and act upon the following advice, which should be worth something, because it is born of much observation, and a large experience. Never rise to speak for the purpose of breaking the silence of a meeting, or filling in the time. Have a distinct thought in your mind when you rise: something definite you want to say, and that you think needs to be said. Say it in your common, plain, every day language, without straining after fine phrases; and be content to stop when you have done, even at the risk of seeming a little abrupt. Lengthy speeches are neither required nor relished in a prayer meeting, and lengthy prayers, as a rule, are not prayers at all. Be sure of this, that with those whose opinion is worth regarding, sincerity will always count for more than grammar and rhetoric.

8. *As far as possible keep strictly to the subject in hand.* Don't wander all over creation. The pastor, if he has done his duty, has come to the meeting with his heart and soul full of a subject, which, if it takes hold of you, and enlists your sympathies and prayers, will profit you. It is your duty to abide by his leading, for he is the shepherd, under Christ, to you. Avoid the bad habit, which some well meaning people have, of always going off on a side track, and starting something new. Keep to what is introduced, and try to see and feel its bearings, and to make others see and feel too. You will thus help to preserve unity of thought and effect. If these simple hints and suggestions are carefully noted, and carried out, they may help a little to make the meeting for prayer what it should be, the most potent agency for good, and the most profitable of all the means of grace.

CHAPTER VII.

The Philosophy of Salvation.

SALVATION is a state of being saved, or a deliverance from some actual or threatened evil, or both, including the present and the future, time and eternity. It is deliverance from sin, including its far reaching consequences, and its vast and overwhelming power. Sin is defined in 1st John, 3 ch., 4 v., as "the transgression of the law," namely, the law of God. Or to put the matter in plain, every day language, with a slight tinge of legal technicality and exactness, sin is a violation of law. That, at least, is one aspect of it, and probably the main one. It is what we call not observing the law, breaking the law. So there cannot be any difficulty in understanding the nature of that terrible evil, in its active form, from which salvation is a deliverance, namely, sin; but there is almost, if not quite, insurmountable difficulty in finding out the why and the wherefore of the evil. Where did it come from? How did it originate? Why did a merciful God permit it? Could He not have prevented it, and if so why did He not?

If my kind and indulgent reader will exercise a little patience I will try to give some sort of an answer to these difficult and constantly recurring questions, and for two reasons. The first is that I have come to think that an answer is possible and practicable, at least approximately so. The second is that we can scarcely understand salvation aright, in its manifold bearings, unless we get some sort of a common sense and consistent idea of the origin of sin, and how it came forth to curse the world, in spite of the loving-kindness and goodness of God.

That sin was anterior to the existence of man on earth we know, for the temptation to it, before which the first pair fell, came from an outside source and agency. It is not, however, with the origin of sin in the universe we are dealing, but with its origin in this world, and its sole relation to man.

That man was made perfect we must take for granted,

and be fully prepared to take it as such notwithstanding the difficulties that may arise in connection with that fact as related to subsequent mutations and events.

Indeed, he must have been perfect, if we admit perfection in God, for he was expressly and designedly made after the Divine image and likeness. "And God said, let us make man in our own image, after our likeness." "So God created man in his own image, in the image of God created he him, male and female created he them." It could not be a physical or form and shape likeness, for it is expressly stated that "The Lord God formed man of the dust of the ground." It was, undoubtedly, a soul likeness, embracing the intellectual, the emotional, and the spiritual; for he "breathed into his nostrils the breath of life, and man became a living soul."

What time elapsed between the creation of the first pair and the fall we are not informed. The main facts alone are given, with just enough detail to intelligently understand and connect them, and this is really all that is necessary. They were created. They had a single restriction imposed upon them by their Creator. They were tempted by a certain agency, in a certain way.

They yielded to temptation, and did what they had been expressly and plainly forbidden to do. They fell, and became actually and painfully conscious of the reality and unworthiness of their disobedience. These are the main facts.

Questions have been asked times without number, and may continue to be asked to the end of time: How could beings made perfect sin? Or why did God issue a command that He must have known they would be successfully tempted to disobey? Or why did He not, in some way best known to His infinite wisdom, successfully interfere to prevent a catastrophe so far-reaching and direful in its consequences?

It would be a perfectly safe, and should be satisfactory, answer to reply, that taking into account all the necessary conditions and circumstances of the case, God could not prevent, or we may presume He would most certainly have done so. This answer, when properly elaborated and understood, really covers the whole ground.

But am I limiting the power of God? Not at all. No man can do that. God only can restrict His own power, and I am simply pointing out, or endeavoring to do so, the limitations which He has created and imposed, and which therefore He cannot pass. We must ever bear in mind that when God crowned the edifice of creation He made a man, and not an automaton; and he would not have been a man, whatever else he might have been, if he had not been endowed with the power to discriminate and choose between good and evil, and right and wrong, involving obedience or disobedience according to his own deliberate choice or will.

Being made in the likeness of God he was necessarily a free agent. His liability to fall was involved in his freedom; his freedom was involved in his moral agency; and his moral agency was his chief glory, and constituted him a man. That God having made him, and made him what he was, a free agent, had a right to put his loyalty to the test, and leave him to his own deliberate choice, whatever the consequences might be, may be regarded as self-evident. What else could he do? To have done otherwise would have been to inflict injustice and degradation upon the highest and noblest work of His hand.

The test itself was neither complex nor difficult, but exceedingly simple and easy. It expressed the whole law of God to them as it then existed; and it was put so plainly that it could not well be misunderstood; "And the Lord God commanded the man, saying, of every tree of the garden thou mayest freely eat; but of the tree of knowledge of good and evil, thou shalt not eat of it; for in the day that thou eatest thereof thou shalt surely die." Gen. 2 ch. 16-17 vs.

That this prohibition applied to Eve, as well as Adam, though subsequently created, is quite clear from subsequent admissions and events. She was the first to acknowledge the prohibition; the first tempted, and the first to yield to temptation and to fall.

The narrative leaves us in no doubt that they both fully undersood the nature of the restriction imposed upon them, and therefore disobedience meant, and could only mean—for they had probably a very high degree of intelligence—that they were not willing to submit themselves, fully and unreservedly, and with an unquestioning faith, to the guidance of God, their Maker and only Friend; and yet it is not at all improable that they had a clear and intelligent idea that their safety and well-being depended upon that. Hence, immediately the fatal transgression was committed they felt guilty, and that before the accusing voice of God was heard. "And the eyes of them both were opened." "And Adam and his wife hid themselves from the presence of the Lord God amongst the trees of the garden." After that God spake to them, and they neither denied nor attempted to justify their disobedience; they simply offered an excuse, and there is always an important difference to be observed between an excuse and a justification. The excuse was that the serpent tempted the woman, and the woman the man. That they, in their inner consciousness, condemned themselves before God pronounced judgment upon them is quite evident.

It would be manifestly unfair, however, not to admit that the temptation was the proximate operating cause of their fall, though it must also be admitted that they might have fallen without it; for the liability to do wrong as well as right is clearly involved in moral agency. Not only then, and now, but for evermore, obedience and disobedience must both be possible to a free agent; for that positively must exist if the freedom be a reality and not a sham. This sufficiently explains, to my mind, the origin of sin, or at least its possible origin, whether in the wide universe of God, or in this world in which we live.

To what extent the race is involved in the first transgression has always been a debatable point. That it is involved, and that very seriously, as far as consequences are concerned, does not admit of doubt, because facts, manifest to all, prove it. But that it is involved to the extent that some people think may, perhaps, be successfully called in question.

That mortality has passed upon all men, as the result of the first sin, cannot be doubted; for it is attested by necessity, by universal experience, and by Scripture. "In the day that thou eatest thereof thou shalt surely die," or as the margin has it, which is more literal and more correct, "dying thou shalt die," was literally fulfilled in the sad experience of the head of our race. From the moment of disobedience the Divine threatening was fulfilled, the seeds of decay and death took root in him; he began to die, and dying was consummated in death, the separation of soul and body.

This mortality has necessarily descended to his posterity. It is inherited from him. But why? Why should I die because he died on account of disobedience? For the simple and all-sufficient reason that it could not be prevented, if the race continued through him. It was simply inevitable. The only way that mortality, with its attendant evils personal and relative, could have been prevented wonld have been by making a posterity impossible, by cutting off humanity at its source. So it was simply a choice between not being at all, or being what we are in regard to death.

Then we have the testimony of universal experience. It is a fact that death has reigned in the world from the beginning, explain it as you may; and it is also a fact that there is a universal expectation and belief that it will continue to the end of time, explain that as you may. We have also the plain attestation of Scripture, especially this, which I am sorry to say has been sadly misinterpreted, and considerably misunderstood: " For as in Adam all die, even so in Christ shall all be made alive." This passage occurs in Paul's sublime and masterly argument about the resurrection of the body, in the fifteenth chapter of his first epistle to the Corinthians, and in the previous verse he says: " For since by man came death, by man came also the resurrection of the dead." Clearly he is speaking of the body in both cases. " By man "—that is, Adam—" came death "; " by man "—that is, Christ—" came also the resurrection of the dead." "In Adam all die; in Christ shall all be made alive." Adam, by his disobedience, made that mortal which was immortal. Christ by His obedience is destined ultimately to make the mortal immortal again. He has brought not only life, but also immortality to light; the first by His death, the second by His obedience, and His own resurrection is the pledge and guarantee. "Because I live, ye shall live also."

The question remains and waits for an answer: Is the race further prejudically affected, and if so, in what manner and to what extent? Here we arrive at a point where theologians part company, and where it becomes us, who value the truth, to look well to our steps, and ponder the path of our feet. Some contend—probably the minority—that the evil resulting from the first transgression, as far as the race is concerned, is confined to mortality, or natural death; and the pains and sorrows, both personal and relative, incident to it. Others contend—and this is probably held by the majority and may be accounted the orthodox belief—that the evil includes not only natural, but also spiritual and eternal death. This is where theologians differ, and where we come to the parting of the way.

Spiritual death is defined as alienation from God. Some are in the habit of defining it as separation from God, but that is a loose and incorrect way of putting it; for the soul, as a matter of fact, can never be separated from God, because God is everywhere; and escape from His presence is impossible. Absolute and complete alienation can exist between two persons, in mind, heart, sympathy, and purpose, though in constant proximity, and dwelling beneath the same roof. So, the soul can be alienated from God, in the most absolute and complete sense, without being separated from Him.

This is not hyper-criticism, for it is really necessary, as far as possible, to correct these inaccurate modes of thought and expression which are altogether too common. I am quite aware that the Psalmist says in one place, "Cast me not away from thy presence," but I am also aware that he says in another place, "Whither shall I flee from thy presence;" and clearly indicating by his subsequent language that he cannot flee from it; for he says: "If I ascend up into heaven, thou art there; if I make my bed in hell, behold thou art there. If I take the wings of the morning, and dwell in the uttermost parts of the sea; even there shall thy hand lead me, and thy right hand shall hold me," Psalm 139, 7-10 vs. So when he says, "Cast me not away from thy presence," he clearly means that separation of soul which is correctly expressed by alienation. True, alienation is separation; that is, it is the cause, and separation is the effect, soul separation. But the popular idea of separation from God partakes a good deal of the geographical. It is taken to mean that God is not only at a great but indefinite distance, which is not the fact; and it is the popular idea, which, being erroneous, we have to correct as far as possible.

And then if we keep this distinction in mind it will not only tend to a more correct apprehension, but it intensifies the thought itself. It shows what alienation is more fully. If you are alienated from a person, and yet for social, business, or any other reasons, you have to spend a good deal of your time in that person's presence, it is a far more irksome and painful thing than if the circumstances were such that you could dispense with the presence of that person altogether. Inevitable proximity adds to the pain and discomfort of your alienation. So it is well to keep this thought constantly in mind that the soul that is alienated from God, and really separated from Him, is still for ever in His presence, from which there is no possible escape.

When theologians speak, as they do, of natural death, spiritual death, and eternal death, some people are apt to think that there is a difference in nature between all three. This is a misapprehension. Between the first and the second there is a difference in nature, the first being the death of the body, and the second the death of the soul. But between the second and the third there is no difference in nature. They are the same. The difference is not in the nature, but in the extension or duration. In short, eternal death is spiritual death indefinitely extended. So that as spiritual death is alienation of the soul from God, eternal death is the indefinite or eternal alienation of the soul from Him. Or, in other words, the one is the same as the other, but it is the projection of the other into the eternal future.

Inasmuch then as the two are identical, apart from the element of duration, they may safely be accounted one as far as the purpose and scope of the present enquiry are concerned. This is the definition in full, of spiritual death I propose to adopt, namely: it is alienation from God, resulting in soul separation; and that this condition, first engendered by the disobedience of Adam, was transmitted, like mortality, as a sad legacy to the race. That as we inherit natural death from Him, so we inherit spiritual death, as inevitably, as literally, and as fully; and so every son and daughter of Adam comes into the world with alienation from God deeply ingrained and implanted in the soul, which time and circumstances in every case, infallibly develop. The alienation may be conscious or unconscious; there may be a lively sense of it, or there may not be; but that does not affect the reality of the condition. It is an indisputable and universal fact.

I suppose we shall be likely to meet at this point precisely the same objections that we have already met in regard to death passing upon all men as the result of the sin of one. People have said, times without number, and many have thought who have not said, that it does not look at all just that people should be born into this world, placed in it without any possibility of consent, and under such unfavorable conditions from the very start.

I am not at all surprised at people who think, having such thoughts, and giving occasional expression to them.

I would be very much surprised if they did not. Such things must come to the surface, sometimes, in any thoughtful mind. Why should I suffer on account of what somebody else did thousands of years ago? Why should I be an unconsenting party to beginning a life under such unfavorable auspices, and with such serious disadvantages and disabilities? Why should I be born into this world, if not in a condemned state from the start, as some people believe and affirm, yet with the moral certainty of my soon assuming such an attitude as will bring me into that condition? Why should I be affected by the sin of another at all, especially to such a serious extent? The all sufficient and only answer to all these questions, which are quite understandable and allowable, is that these things are so, because, under the conditions and circumstances, they could not be otherwise. When we meet with the inevitable, it is wisdom to submit.

We must bear in mind that the law of cause and effect was just as operative then as it is now; and law, and especially this law, is evermore inexorable, and will not be entreated. As it was threatened so it came to pass that disobedience wrought a great and marvellous physical and moral change in our progenitors, and if the race must continue through them it was inevitable, as inevitable as the operation of cause and effect, that their physical and moral characteristics and disabilities must be inherited.

Do I mean that sin is transmitted? I do not. I have, I hope, too much regard for common sense to make any statement that can fairly bear any such construction. Sin cannot be transmitted, because all moral distinctions must be subverted to achieve such a result as that ; but the condition, or nature, or bias, or whatever else you choose to call it, that may produce sin, can be transmitted ; and it is capable of precisely the same proof as the transmission of mortality, namely necessity, experience, and scripture. There was simply a choice between non-existence, by cutting off humanity at its source, and thus preventing a posterity, or existence under such conditions as we have, unpleasant and undesirable as they are in some respects.

God must have thought that the latter was better for humanity, and for His own glory, than the former, and all right thinking persons will be likely to concur in the wisdom of the Divine choice. Non-existence is nothing ;

existence is something, even under unfavorable conditions; and it has before it endless possibilities of good under the Divine plan. It does at least give the chance of holding what is, with a fair prospect of gaining all, or perhaps more, than was lost.

It may, however, be objected to this process of reasoning that the alternative referred to was not the only possible one under the circumstances. By which is meant, I suppose, that it was not absolutely necessary to continue the race in the projected and now vitiated line; but that God might have allowed Adam and Eve to perish in their sin with no hope or chance of posterity; and then have created another pair, equally innocent and perfect, who might more successfully stand the test of obedience to their Maker, and thus become the head of an obedient and perfect race of beings.

This suggestion or objection, whichever you choose to call it, may seem, to some people, trivial, but I am not disposed to regard it in that light. I think it is reasonable and worth consideration, and if a fairly satisfactory answer can be had it should be forthcoming. The main thing to determine, as far as possible, is: What are the reasonable probabilities in the supposed contingency that is submitted for consideration? I think they are the following; at least, they are so far as they appear to me. Suppose God had done as suggested, destroyed the first pair after their disobedience, and prevented all possibility of increase along that line; and suppose He had created others with like nature and endowments, and submitted them to the same test? What would have been the likely result?

To my mind there is not a shadow of probability that the result of the second trial would have been different from the first. Of course, it is purely a matter of conjecture in a supposed case, but this is the only basis of reasoning which such a case admits of. We must reason this way, or not reason at all. That is, the fact of the first pair falling furnishes a reasonable conjecture that the second would be more likely to incur the same fate than not to incur it; especially in view of the fact that they would be of the same nature, and would be put to the same test, having, as moral agents, the same liability to fall, and the same temptations to it. Granted the same nature, the same conditions, and the same circumstances, the result would be more likely to be the same than to be different.

But you ask, could not God make a man without his being liable to fall? The answer is that both experience and reason say no, and that emphatically.

A man cannot be a man, without being a free agent, and free agency means liberty and ability to discriminate and choose; and choice, if it be a reality and not a sham, necessarily involves—while right and wrong exist—the liability to choose either in preference to the other; and this power, which involves such a liability, is, and must ever remain, the strength and weakness, and the glory and danger of a moral being.

We have been concerned so far, in this enquiry, with the nature rather than the precise extent of the moral damage inflicted upon the race by the first transgression. In the fifth chapter of the epistle to the Romans the extent is defined and illustrated with more amplitude and precision than anywhere else; and the summing up of the whole is given in the nineteenth verse where we have the somewhat startling statement: "For as by one man's disobedience many were made sinners, so by the obedience of one shall many be made righteous."

Please to observe this statement very closely. There is no ambiguity about it, and there is nothing in the original, nor in any manuscript authorities, to suggest or warrant any alteration in the terms or meaning. We must take it just as it is, and try to understand it as well as we can, though at the first blush it seems to conflict with our reason. I say it seems so; I don't say it does. I am anxious that the reader should be very particular in noticing what is said in this connection, for this reason, that, I frankly confess, if I had met the first part of the Apostle's statement anywhere except in a book which I believe to be inspired, I should have been disposed to reject it as untrue, as something that could not be. Why? Because according to the ordinary meaning and use of language, it looks like a point blank declaration of the transmission of sin; and as a matter of fact sin cannot be transmitted, because to admit the possibility of such a thing would be to admit that man's moral nature and all moral distinctions can be entirely and absolutely subverted. In other words, it would be admitting the possibility of a moral impossibility.

Two things, of some importance, should be noticed here before we proceed further. First, whatever the "many" means in the first part must logically and reasonably be accepted as its meaning in the second.

Common seuse and fairness will preclude anyone saying that "many" means all in the first part and only a part in the second. It cannot be taken as universal in one case, and limited in the other. It must be either one or the other in both cases. Therefore we are shut up to the conclusion that it is universal in both cases, for we know the first is universal because all, and not a part, are involved in the consequences of "one man's disobedience." So also the all, and not a part, are, in some sense, partakers of the benefits accruing from the obedience of Christ.

Then again, observe that he says: "For as by one man's disobedience many were made sinners." There is a very important and even fundamental difference between that and saying that many were made sinful, which is about all that reason seems prepared to admit.

This simple consideration places before us in its true light, and in its full magnitude, the difficulty we have to meet in the statement we are considering ; and we must make some attempt to harmonize it with the dictates of reason, and with our ordinary ideas of what is possible and just. We naturally, and very properly, ask: How can one man's sin make another man a sinner, and especially how can it make an innumerable number of sinners? And even if it could be done, which seems— I say seems—morally impossible, where would be the justice of it, as we understand justice?

In answering these questions, which are quite allowable and reasonable, and endeavoring to show that the statement of the Apostle is both possible and just, we must bear in mind that much, if not all, depends upon what we understand by sin, and how we define it. Sin is a biblical term and expresses a biblical idea, something, in fact, peculiar to the Bible. The Bible is our sole and only authority upon that subject. It is there we learn all about it; its origin, nature, progress and effects. We must therefore let the Bible speak for itself, and let it inform us as to what sin is, if we would judge rightly of its effects. We can scarcely expect to come to a right conclusion unless we accept the definition, or definitions, it gives.

I find four distinct definitions of sin in the New Testament. The first is Romans, 14 ch. 23 v. : "For whatsover is not of faith is sin." The immediate and local application of this need not concern us, for whatever that may be we have here a definition of sin. Faith is belief, and belief is the opposite of unbelief, and therefore unbelief is sin. Unbelief represents character, and is a condition of mind and heart. Observe, it is a condition. This is confirmed by Romans, 8 ch. 6-7 vs. "To be carnally minded is death." "The carnal mind is enmity against God." So it is clear that a certain moral condition or state is in itself sin according to these definitions.

The second definition is in James, 4 ch. 17 v., "Therefore to him that knoweth to do good, and doeth it not, to him it is sin." According to this, sin is negative, and although negative it is a step in advance of the other, which is simply a condition or state. It is sin not to do good, when knowledge, and power, and opportunity are possessed for doing it. Failing to do right is sin. Not doing what we are told to do is just as literally sin as doing what we are told not to do. The one is disobedience as well as the other, and has its appropriate penalty attached. "And that servant, which knew his lord's will, and prepared not himself, neither did according to his will, shall be beaten with many stripes." Luke, 12 ch. 47 v.

The third definition is that which is best known, and

most frequently quoted in 1st John, 3 ch., 4 v., "Whosoever committeth sin transgresseth also the law, for sin is the transgression of the law." This is positive and refers to the express violation of specific enactments. This is sin in its commonest and most definite form. It is a violation of law. It is positive disobedience.

The fourth definition is in 1st John, 5 ch., 17 v., "All unrighteousness is sin." We have nothing to do with these words in their specific connection, in the present enquiry. We simply have to do with them as giving us a definition of sin; and in that they are not at all ambiguous, but very explicit. The definition is comprehensive. It sums up the other three. Unrighteousness is what is morally wrong in all its forms and manifestations, and therefore it includes character and condition, as well as conduct in its negative and positive aspects. If I speak of an unrighteous man I may have reference to his character, or his conduct, or both. I may mean that unrighteousness expresses the character he bears, or his moral condition or state; or I may mean that he acts unrighteously; or both ideas may be included in my statement. So that we arrive at this conclusion, from these scriptural definitions, that sin is condition as well as action, character as well as conduct, negative as well as positive.

It will now be apparent to any one reading these pages that if the Bible contained no other definition of sin than that of its being the "transgression of the law," it would be impossible to harmonize the statement of the Apostle with reason and common sense, and with our ordinary ideas of what is possible and just. Because, what I must, for the sake of distinction, call positive sin, cannot be transmitted; for that would involve a complete subversion of man's moral nature, and all moral distinctions; neither can it harmonize with our ideas of what is morally possible or just to suppose that one man's sin can make another man a sinner—much less a whole race—in the positive sense of the term.

Fortunately we are not obliged to adopt the wild theories that have been promulgated upon this subject, and that lead to all sorts of moral contradictions and absurdities; which theories may have had their origin in the forgetfulness of the fact that there is more than one definition of sin in the Bible. Sin, as expressing a certain moral condition, may be taken as the initial and primal thought, and the first stage of development; and taking this, which is the first biblical definition, as the basis of our exegesis of Paul's famous statement, concerning the effect of the first act of disobedience upon the race, we are warranted in stating that the Apostle means that Adam transmitted to his posterity the moral condition of alienation from the Life of God which sin produced in him. And this was inevitable, just as inevitable as the transmission of mortality through him to his posterity.

There is nothing arbitrary in this, and I fail to see that there is any thing punitive. It is simply the working out of the inexorable law of cause and effect. It was inevitable that the race, descending from him, would inherit his physical and moral characteristics and disabilities.

The question that calls for our careful consideration now, is,—and it is an important one and a wide one—How, in what manner, and to what extent does the obedience of Christ repair, meet, or rectify the moral damage inflicted upon the race by the disobedience of Adam? We are bound—as we have already observed—by the laws of fair interpretation, and of common sense, to admit that what "many" means in one case, in Rom. 5 ch. 19 v., it also means in the other; that they are, in fact, co-extensive; and we should be prepared to admit this, frankly and fearlessly, because it seems to us right, whatever the logical outcome may be. And what is the logical outcome? As far as I can see it is simply this: that as the whole race is related to and affected by the disobedience of Adam, so the whole race is affected by and stands in an important relation to the obedience of Christ. The one was meant by Divine wisdom to be an exact counterpoise of the other. No sooner was the fall an accomplished fact, the race involved, and the damage to the race potentially done, than the promise of the effective counterpoise was immediately issued, in which the race was equally involved, and the good to the race potentially done. "And I will put enmity between thee and the woman, and between thy seed and her seed; it shall bruise thy head, and thou shalt bruise his heel." Gen. 3 ch. 15 v. From that moment the obedience of Christ was a potential fact, and immediately operative for the benefit of the race, according to the Divine purpose, and in the Divine mind. So there was no delay in providing an effective remedy, and that remedy was at once available; available for the first transgressors, and for all their posterity.

When we speak of the obedience of Christ we must bear in mind its important relation to His death. "He humbled himself, and became obedient unto death, even the death of the cross," Phil. 2 ch., 8 v. The cross was the climax of His obedience. It was the highest point, the severest test, and the most signal manifestation. Higher than divesting Himself of His glory; higher than coming to earth; higher than the humiliation of His humble birth and life; higher than His voluntary servitude; higher than His sufferings and privations; higher than the agony and bloody sweat of Gethsemane. It was higher than all these, and His voluntary submission to it was the crowning act of His obedient life. Yes, the crowning act, and, merciful heavens! what a sight it was. What a spectacle for men and angels! What an object lesson to stamp itself upon the imagination of the ages! How humiliating the associations; how excruciating the pain; how disgraceful the mode, that reserved for the worst criminals. And oh! that hideous vulgarity, and that mortal hate that gleamed from those Jewish eyes. The worst passions were dominant in that infuriated mob. How they jested, and sneered, and mercilessly heaped one indignity after another upon the

Almighty victim. Hell was let loose. No wonder creation shuddered, and the earth shook, and the graves were opened, and the veil of the temple and the rocks were rent. No wonder that the heavens put on sackcloth, and that "there was darkness over all the land." And oh! that startled, piercing, agonizing cry, which must have touched and moved the very throne of the Eternal, as it has touched and moved millions of human hearts: "Eli, Eli, lama, sabachthani; that is to say, My God, My God, why hast thou forsaken me." "When he had cried again with a loud voice, he yielded up the ghost." This was obedience, obedience unto death, even the death of the cross.

We may well enquire, What has this obedience and death accomplished for the race? It has accomplished two things, and by accomplishing these, it has proved an exact moral counterpoise of the disobedience of Adam. What are they? The first is, that it has brought immortality to light. Adam's disobedience brought mortality into the world. Christ's obedience restores the balance in that particular, and restores it for the whole race. "For since by man came death, by man came also the resurrection of the dead; for as in

Adam all die, even so in Christ shall all be made alive." 1 Cor., 15 ch. 21-22 vs. The plain and obvious meaning is that in and through Adam we all die, and in and through Christ we shall all be made alive,—raised from the dead.

The second benefit that Christ's obedience unto death has secured for the race is, that it has made atonement for sin. He died for all. All are included in the scope of the great and merciful plan. Not one is left out, from the first to the last. The mighty sweep of that marvellous obedience takes them all in. It is the rainbow of promise and hope for a lost world. It contains the germinal principle, which, in its gradual but unceasing development, will ultimately sweep away the mighty wreck that sin has made, acquire universal dominion, and re-constitute all things upon a firm and enduring basis; even to the extent of a new heaven and a new earth, when the first heaven and the first earth are passed away.

The universality of the atonement should be accepted as placed beyond all doubt by the following explicit statements: "All we like sheep have gone astray; we have turned every one to his own way; and the Lord hath laid on him the iniquity of us all." Isaiah, 53 ch. 6 v, "For the love of Christ constraineth us, because we thus judge, that if one died for all then were all dead; and that he died for all, that they which live should not, henceforth, live unto themselves, but unto him which died for them and rose again." 2 Cor. 5 ch. 14-15 vs. "We see Jesus, who was made a little lower than the angels for the suffering of death, crowned with glory and honor; that He by the grace of God, should *taste death for every man.*" Heb. 2 ch. 9 v. "And he is the propitiation for our sins, and not for ours only, but also *for the sins of the whole world.*" 1 John, 2 ch. 2 v.

The last two statements, especially, must evermore be accepted, by all reasonable minds, as placing beyond any possibility of doubt the universality of the atonement; that Christ died not simply to put away sin, but died with full, loving, sacrificing intent and purpose for every son and daughter of Adam; and that He secured two things for every one, a potential immortality which will become actual at the resurrection—of which His own is the pledge—and a condition of potential salvation, which can be made actual by simple acquiesence. And thus all mankind, from the first man to the last, saved or unsaved, are left without any just ground of complaint regarding the inevitable effects produced by the first transgression.

A question may arise here, in any thoughtful and logical mind, and which had better, as far as possible, be met at once, as a more favorable opportunity may not occur. Having established an equality of effect—the one exactly meeting the other—between the disobedience of Adam and the obedience of Christ upon the race; the one creating and entailing mortality, the other destroying it in His own person; the one entailing a condition of sin, the other creating and introducing to a condition of salvation; what about the effects resulting from the inevitable development of both conditions? Are they equal, or does justice require that they should be? I think not, for the latter case, which is supposed, and concerning which the query is made, is fundamentally different from the former. How different from the former you may ask?

I answer, different in this, that in the former, man's attitude is passive, while in the latter it is active. In the former we have nothing to do with the production of the effects, in the latter we have everything to do.

In the former choice does not come into operation, in the latter it does. In other words, we had nothing to do with creating the dual condition in which we find ourselves, in regard to sin on the one hand, and salvation on the other; but our moral agency, or choice, comes into operation in the development of both. Therefore, while the conditions created for us are equal, the one balancing the other, the results of their development—dependent as they are upon choice—may be disproportionate, without in any wise reflecting upon the goodness and justice of God.

So then both conditions are potential, and can not be anything else in view of the free agency of man; and they are equal, as far as we can see; and both may be converted from the potential into the actual by the action of the human will.

Whatever the environment of a free agent may be, he sins because he wills to sin. In fact no action can be sin, as far as the actor is personally concerned, without the free action of the will. So on the other hand in regard to salvation, where the necessary knowledge is possessed, a man accepts or rejects; and the acceptance or the rejection is the result of the operation of the will.

If he accepts, he is justified and saved. If he rejects—knowingly, consciously, wilfully rejects, he is already in a state of condemnation; not for his sin—for that has been atoned for, and salvation is potentially his upon the basis of that atonement—but for his rejection. Faith, which is a personal appropriation and use of the benefit conferred, saves. Unbelief, which is a failure to so appropriate and use the benefit, is condemnation.

To show the correctness of this view a number of passages of scripture might be given, but it is not necessary as they are quite familiar to the intelligent reader of the Bible, or they can easily be found by any one who has any interest in this enquiry. Just a few must suffice here, and I will confine myself to the words of Christ, than whom no one could be better qualified to speak on this subject, for He is the fountain of truth. The third chapter of John's gospel—which, next to the Sermon on the Mount, is perhaps the most important and remarkable exposition of spiritual truth that Christ ever gave—contains all the references that we need to make our contention plain. Take verses 14, 15, 16, 18 and 36 "And as Moses lifted up the serpent in the wilderness, even so must the Son of Man be lifted up; that whosoever believeth in Him should not perish, but have eternal life." "For God so loved the world, that He gave His only begotten Son, that whosoever believeth in Him should not perish but have eternal life." "He that believeth in Him is not condemned; but he that believeth not is condemned already, because he hath not believed in the name of the only begotten Son of God." "He that believeth on the Son hath everlasting life; and he that believeth not the Son shall not see life, but the wrath of God abideth on him." The last two verses present the grand alternative in its full and complete form, and the former of these two is remarkably full and very precise, admitting of no possible chance of mistaking or perverting the meaning: "He that believeth not is condemned already, because he hath not believed."

It is a melancholy reflection, that rich and all sufficient as the provision for man's need is—wide as the world, and extensive as the fall—more than half the whole of mankind cannot, from a variety of causes, make a personal appropriation of that provision. I allude to infants who die before attaining the position of moral accountability; those who are mentally incapable; and all to whom the knowledge of Christ and His salvation has not come; and by the latter I mean those who have had no opportunity of receiving that knowledge.

It will at once be seen that we are approaching a difficult aspect of the subject, the relation of the three classes mentioned to salvation. What is it, and what the effect of that relationship?

Of the different theories propounded in regard to infant salvation, which I am unable to accept, there is only one which I propose to notice, namely, that all infants dying before committing actual sin do not need salvation by Christ. To dispose of this by showing that it cannot be maintained is not difficult. If Christ died for all He died for them, and if He died for them there was certainly a needs be for His doing so. Furthermore they inherit a corrupt nature inevitably, just as inevitably as they inherit mortality; and when this begins to manifest itself it shows a strong likeness to the first transgression; for, as the first sin was insubordination, or a revolt against God's authority, so the first manifestation of a child's will, invariably takes the shape of resistance to constituted

—parental—authority. I conclude that infants need saving, and that they can only be saved through Christ.

With reference to the second class, the mentally incapable, it may be as well to explain that those are meant who are so far incapacitated as not only to affect but to cut off their moral accountability. Of course there are different causes, and degrees, and duration of incapacity, which enter into the absolute determination of cases, but into these we do not propose to enter

With reference to the heathen, who are comprehended in the third class, those only are meant who have had no opportunity of coming to a knowledge of Christ and His salvation.

I am fully aware—and perhaps it may be as well to give a passing notice to this—that when people ask about the unenlightened heathen, in regard to salvation, it is usual to refer them to what Paul says in his epistle to the Romans, 2 ch. 12-15 vs. If you will take the trouble to look and read carefully you will find nothing there about salvation. In fact, the whole chapter is taken up with reasoning about human conduct, and the particular portion referred to is intended to prove what the apostle states in the eleventh verse, that, "there is no respect of persons with God" He is taking the self-righteous, proud Jew down from his high and self-assumed position, by telling him that God will not discriminate in his favor. He will be just to all, and Jew and Gentile alike will be judged by Him according to the light and knowledge possessed.

With the view of making some contribution to a possible solution of the grave and important problem we are considering, namely, the salvation of infants, the mentally incapable, and all to whom—through no fault of theirs—the knowledge of Christ and His salvation has not come, I submit the following propositions. They are in regular sequence, and lead to an inevitable conclusion.

1. That Christ died for all, which means every son and daughter of Adam, from the first to the last.

2. Therefore His death is co-extensive with the fall of man.

3. Therefore there is no need of any other salvation, or any other method of restoring fallen humanity, under any circumstances, to the life and favor of God.

4. Therefore there is no salvation out of Christ, as the scripture saith: "Neither is there salvation in any

other, for there is none other name, under heaven, given among men, whereby we must be saved." Acts, 4 ch., 12 v.

5. What is provided for all cannot be denied to any, except those who knowingly and wilfully reject.

6. Knowledge of an obligation is necessary to its performance.

7. Ability to perform an obligation is necessary to the just requirement of its performance.

8. God is just

9. God cannot be unjust.

10. Therefore God cannot require the impossible.

11. Infants, who have not attained to the necessary knowledge and moral responsibility; the mentally incapable, whose condition is such as to cut off moral responsibility; and all who have not come to a knowledge of Christ and what He has done, can neither accept nor reject salvation.

12. Therefore the salvation provided for all must take effect, in all the cases, where absolute inability to accept exists, except where the inability is the result of personal fault.

It may be objected to these propositions, and the inevitable conclusion to which they lead, that they seem to make practically unnecessary the preaching of the gospel to the heathen. To this objection, fair and reasonable as it seems to be, the Great Commission is an all-sufficient answer: "Go ye into all the world and preach the gospel to every creature." No consideration, no series of considerations, can, in any wise, or to any extent, successfully interfere with the discharge of a paramount obligation like that. It may furthermore be contended that what the Psalmist calls "the joy of salvation" is something worth having; and this, it is clearly evident, is only possible to the conscious recipient of the great benefit. Besides, there is the advantage of consecrated service, and of growing up into the life of Christ, and a consequent fuller capacity and meetness for the service and life of heaven. All these are great and manifest advantages that grow out of the conscious possession and exercise of salvation. They are of considerable value here, and they project themselves, with increasing force and worth, into the eternal future.

It may also be objected that upon the basis of the conclusion reached by the propositions, we may inflict irreparable damage upon many in the heathen world by taking the gospel to them, inasmuch that while many may accept, many will likely not; and these, by rejection, will be placed in a worse position than they would have been if left in entire ignorance of the gospel scheme.

It is quite sufficient to say in answer to this, that if the objection is valid at all it will equally apply to the preaching of the gospel anywhere, in any country, or in any age; for the gospel is not only a saving but also a condemning power, wherever it is proclaimed, according to the acquiescence or non-acquiescence of those to whom it is made known.

Paul, referring to the effects of his own preaching (2 Cor., 2 ch., 16 v.) says: "To the one the savour of death unto death; and to the other the savour of life unto life." And then he adds—with an evident feeling of great responsibility at the thought of being instrumental, in some measure, of the condemnation of some, by their rejection of the gospel which he preached to them—"And who is sufficient for these things." He did not, however, forbear to preach on that account.

Having noticed these objections, let us return to the

main question, to present some considerations confirmatory of the soundness of the conclusion we have reached, in regard to the salvation of the three classes referred to.

1. We may be tolerably sure that we are on the line of truth, when we do not violate sound reason and common sense, in dealing with matters upon which the Bible is either silent, or not entirely explicit.

2. We are certainly on the line of a true conception of the Divine character and intentions, when the tendency of our reasoning, being in itself sound, is in the direction of enlarging our views of the exceeding wideness of the Divine mercy; for God certainly intends to include all, in the scope and benefits of His gracious plan, who do not *wilfully* and *responsibly* exclude themselves.

3. If it be maintained that God intended that non-acquiescence should be an effectual bar to the possession and enjoyment of His mercy, in every case, and under all circumstances, we must conclude either that He is unjust in dealing with His creatures, or that His plan is a partial failure, which would be a serious reflection upon His wisdom.

4. Had God intended that there should be no exception to the rule, as to the prescribed acquiescence, it is impossible to resist the conclusion that He would, by some agency, within His competence, have made the knowledge of the facts, and the opportunities and power of compliance, as universal as the obligation to believe.

5. If only those can be saved who have a knowledge of, and exercise a conscious faith in Christ, infants and incapables are as effectually excluded from a participation in the benefits of the gracious plan, as those to whom, from no fault of theirs, the knowledge of Christ has not come. And no one but a monster, or one who thinks that God is such, could for a moment entertain the belief that infants and incapables are, for non-acquiescence, which they cannot avoid, shut out from the Divine mercy.

Let us be thankful that God's plan is larger than man's mind. He is juster and more merciful than we are, and more merciful because He is more just. It was an act of Sovereignty in Him not to cut off the race at its source, after the first transgression; for He willed it so, and will and action in Him are necessarily synonymous and simultaneous.

It was an act of justice in Him to provide an efficient and exact counterpoise for that condition which the posterity of Adam had nothing to do with creating; and upon that foundation He has built that marvellous structure of "grace and truth," which, as far as we know, is the solitary moral wonder of the universe. With Him, justice and mercy are not opposing and contradictory terms, for in His being and nature there is nothing contradictory. From His justice we see the outflow of His mercy, and when we behold His mercy we see His justice too. God's character is perfectly harmonious, though made up of separate and constituent parts or attributes, which, like the colors of the rainbow, blend, and form a wondrous arch of beauty, of promise, and of hope. O! when will men understand how good God is, and how deeply and unalterably He loves them.

He is not exclusive; He is inclusive. That is His nature, and the whole bent and energy of that nature. He is concerned to save His erring, lost children, not to condemn them; and no heart can reach out to Him, however feebly, but will find itself encompassed by the Everlasting Arms. He who knew the heart of God, as no one else did or can, said: "For God sent not His

Son into the world to condemn the world, but that the world through Him might be saved." John, 3 ch., 17 v.

> "There's a wideness in God's mercy,
> Like the wideness of the sea;
> There's a kindness in His justice,
> Which is more than liberty.
>
> There is welcome for the sinner,
> And more graces for the good;
> There is mercy with the Saviour;
> There is healing in His blood.
>
> For the love of God is broader
> Than the measure of man's mind;
> And the heart of the Eternal
> Is most wonderfully kind.
>
> If our love were but more simple,
> We should take Him at His word;
> And our lives would be all sunshine
> In the sweetness of our Lord."

CHAPTER VIII.

The Duty of Supporting the Gospel.

THIS is a very practical subject, and its importance will be immediately and fully recognized. Of course pecuniary support is meant. There are other kinds of support, which Christians may and do render to the Gospel, but the pecuniary is that aspect of it—and a very important one—which will be considered in this chapter.

Here, be it observed that this specific support which the Gospel needs, in order to its propagation, is the foundation of all human instrumentality. We cannot work without tools. We cannot successfully conduct a warfare without weapons. We cannot overthrow the enemy, so far as his overthrow depends upon human endeavor, without the necessary appliances. The Gospel cannot be propagated without keeping the Divinely ordained human machinery going.

God, perhaps, might have converted the world without any human instrument; but inasmuch as He has seen fit, in His infinite wisdom, to honor us by ordering it otherwise, we must fall in with the plan, and render all the support that is needed, on our part, to its proper and efficient execution.

The duty we are considering may therefore be regarded as enforced by *the necessity of the case.* I mean by necessity neither chance nor fate, but that which has been, evidently, ordained by Divine wisdom. God has seen fit to make us, who are human, co-workers with Himself in the accomplishment of His merciful purposes oncerning men. The human instrumentality is as Divinely ordained as the Divine agency, and therefore on that account as necessary, though not as efficient, in the accomplishment of the result contemplated. We see the combination—and, indeed, the expressly designed combination—of these two agencies, human and Divine, in the Great Commission: "Go ye therefore, and *teach all nations.* . . . . and lo *I am with you alway.*"

It was not the preaching of Peter, or the working of the Holy Spirit, contemplated separately, which produced the stupendous result of the conversion of "three thousand souls" on the day of Pentecost. It was the combination of the two. It was the working of the Divine, all-subduing power, through spiritual truth, presented by a human instrument. It is to be observed, however, that the human instrument, concerned in this work, unlike the Divine agent, is so constituted, and its necessities and surroundings are such, that it needs human support as well as Divine aid. It cannot exist, work, nor grow in working without it. It is made indispensable by a Divine ordinance. It should be enough to say, in plain words, that God has made it so, and it is not for us to neglect or, in any wise, alter the Divine plan. His ways are not only higher, but better than our ways, and His thoughts than our thoughts.

Those who contend for the gospel being free are right. It is free in its essential nature, made free, and free to all. That is the genius of the gospel. But those who contend for a ministration of the gospel, which involves no charge, are blind to the teachings of common sense, human experience, and the Divine word. They are like a man, who because he can get the clear, sparkling water from its mountain source for nothing, will, on that account, insist upon having a pitcher, in which to carry it to his home, for nothing too. Or to slightly vary the illustration; water is free, free enough, and there is certainly enough to make it free, as far as the simple element itself is concerned. You can go down to the free flowing river and get as much as you like, and probably no one will say you nay. Under no circumstances do you pay for the water, that being God's free gift to all His creatures alike, but you may have to pay for the appliances and expenditure involved in bringing it to your homes, and rightly so too.

So the Gospel is free, as free as anything in God's creation can be, free as air, free as water; but inasmuch as there is a human instrument employed, and necessarily employed, in conveying it to man, we must pay for the instrument, and it is certainly reasonable that we should do so. And then the Scriptures are neither silent nor ambiguous upon this matter. Indeed, they are very explicit, and exceedingly plain. There is no mistaking the meaning. The quotations following are from Paul's epistles, and Paul was well qualified to speak upon this subject, for he was not only inspired to declare the mind of God, but he was also remarkably, and, we have reason to believe, exceptionally disinterested.

While not allowing himself, for reasons which he plainly states, to become a burden to the churches, he never allowed them to call in question the right of the laborer to an adequate support. "Who goeth a warfare, at any time, at his own charges? Who planteth a vineyard, and eateth not of the fruit thereof? Or who feedeth a flock, and eateth not of the milk of the flock? Say I these things as a man, or saith not the law the same also? For it is written in the law of Moses, thou shalt not muzzle the mouth of the ox that treadeth out the corn. Doth God take care for oxen? Or saith he it altogether for our sakes? For our sakes, no doubt, this is written; that he that ploweth should plow in hope; and that he that thresheth in hope should be partaker of his hope. If we have sown unto you spiritual things, is it a great thing if we shall reap your carnal things? If others be partakers of this power over you, are not we rather? Nevertheless we have not used this power, but suffer all things, lest we should hinder the Gospel of Christ. Do ye not know that they which minister about holy things live of the things of the temple? And they which wait at the altar are partakers with the altar? Even so hath

the Lord ordained that they which preach the Gospel should live of the gospel." 1 Cor. 9 ch. 7-14 vs.
"Let him that is taught in the word communicate unto him that teacheth in all good things." Gal. 6 ch. 6 v. "Let the elders that rule well be counted worthy of double honor, especially they who labor in the word and doctrine. For the Scripture saith, thou shalt not muzzle the ox that treadeth out the corn; and the laborer is worthy of his reward." 1 Tim. 5 ch. 17-18 vs.

This duty of supporting the gospel is further enforced by the consideration of stewardship. We are "stewards of the manifold grace of God." What we have is entrusted to us, and not for our benefit alone. There are two plain propositions which every Christian will fully and readily admit. The first is that every good gift cometh from God. The second is that the things which come from Him should be disposed of according to His will, so far as that will can be ascertained.

Accumulation may be the law of man, but distribution is the law of God. "Freely ye have received, freely give."

Getting money honestly, and for definite and good purposes, is a virtue, but getting it for the mere purpose of accumulation, and with the view of personal enjoyment and benefit only, is a sin, and that because it is opposed to the law of the Giver of all Good, namely distribution. The man who, in any way, impedes the circulation of God's gifts, commits more than a mistake; he commits a sin, for which he will most certainly be called to account. That any human creature should want for any temporal benefit, or spiritual gift, is no reflection upon God. The want does not arise from any inadequacy in the supply, but from a lack of proper and efficient distribution. It is a failure in stewardship. There is certainly enough for all, at all times, and if the due proportion which each needs fails to reach each one, some one is blameworthy. What we, in our personal capacity, really need—and God is the judge of that—of temporal and spiritual things are ours; all that we are possessed of beyond that belongs to the needy; and we are culpable, or they are, or it may be a measure of culpability attaches to both, if it fails to reach them.

In truth, we receive God's gifts for our own needs and enjoyment, and for the need and enjoyment of others. It is both a mistake and a sin when a man, and especially a Christian man, stops short at himself, and fails to consider the condition and claims of his fellow men. A stream will furnish the moving power for a hundred mills as well as one, if you let it flow on in its natural course. You will get all you need out of it, and it will be a benefit and blessing to others without in any wise impoverishing you.

We receive light that we may shine for the benefit of others, and the glory of God. " Ye are the light of the world. A city that is set on a hill cannot be hid. Neither do men light a candle, and put it under a bnshel but on a candlestick ; and it giveth light unto all that are in the house. Let your light so shine before men, that they may see your good works, and glorify your Father which is in heaven." Matt., 5 ch., 14-16 v.

Knowledge is given to us—and especially Divine knowledge—that we may enjoy it ourselves, and instruct others, and in giving we always receive the more. We receive comfort from the Divine source, not for our own advantage only, but also that we may comfort them who are in any sorrow.

We are prospered in our worldly concerns, our substance is increased, partly for our own advantage, but mainly that we may become the ministers of good to others; especially in the spreading abroad of that gospel without which the world, at its best, is a blank, death is a terror, and eternity is a darkness awful and indescribable.

The Apostle lays down this principle very simply and very effectively in the twelfth chapter of his Epistle to the Romans: "Having then gifts differing according to the grace that is given to us; whether prophecy, let us prophesy according to the proportion of faith; or ministry, let us wait on our ministering; or he that teacheth, on teaching; or he that exhorteth, on exhortation; he that giveth, let him do it with simplicity; he that ruleth, with dilligence; he that showeth mercy, with cheerfulness."

This truth is not sufficiently recognized, though it is here implied in the plainest inferential manner, that a Christian man who is blessed with wealth is as responsible for giving to the fullest extent of his power, for the propagation of the Gospel, as the minister who is endowed with the gift of prophesying is responsible for preaching the Gospel to the full measure of the ability granted to him. We plead for the development, to the largest possible extent, of the efficacy of the pulpit, and rightly so too; but let it not be forgotten that there is a corresponding duty incumbent upon the occupants of the pew. Let there be a holy rivalry in giving and working. Let there be a real and earnest contention, not as to which can do the least, but which can do the most, for the Master and His cause. If the gifts of teaching and preaching are to be increasingly developed, let the gift of temporal means be increasingly developed too. Let the servants of Christ teach with all their power, preach with all their power, and give to the full extent of their power. Give, till you feel it. Give, till giving becomes a sacrifice. If you give till you are poor, you will only be faintly approximating the example of your Divine Lord, who, "though He was rich, yet for your sakes He became poor, that ye through His poverty might be rich."

This duty is further enforced by certain prudential considerations. It is not only wise, but it pays to give the gospel a liberal support. A whole-souled liberality often has its reward, even in kind, in this life. "There is that scattereth, and yet increaseth, and there is that withholdeth more than is meet, but it tendeth to poverty. The liberal soul shall be made fat, and he that watereth shall be watered also himself." Prov., 11 ch., 24-25 vs. "Honour the Lord with thy substance, and with the first fruits of all thine increase; so shall thy barns be filled with plenty, and thy presses shall burst out with new wine." Prov., 3 ch., 9-10 vs. "But this I say, he which soweth sparingly shall reap also sparingly; and he which soweth bountifully shall reap also bountifully. Every man according as he purposeth in his heart, so let him give; not grudgingly, or of necessity, for God loveth a cheerful giver." 2nd Cor., 9 ch., 6.7 vs.

Nature exemplifies this law of increase. Every farmer knows, or should know, that the earth yields its fruit, to a large extent, according to the care bestowed upon it. Liberal expenditure in cleaning, tilling, ploughing, seeding, and any other necessary operations, will produce liberal crops; while a niggardly expenditure, and want of proper care and attention, will be apt to produce very small and unsatisfactory results. The earth will use you as you use it. If you are liberal, it will be profuse. If you are parsimonious it will pay you back in your own coin.

Business exemplifies this law of increase. Many a man

has suffered a considerable loss by parsimoniously avoiding a little judicious expenditure. Here is a man who has a valuable property. He thinks he will save the insurance money by taking extra care. He goes on all right for a time. He saves a hundred, two hundred, or perhaps five hundred dollars, and then, notwithstanding his extra care, the fire fiend comes, and sweeps all away. The poor, thrifty man has perhaps saved five hundred dollars, and lost ten thousand. He withheld more than was meet, and it tended to poverty.

The man who succeeds in business is he who has full capacity and is wise, and at the same time has daring enough to launch out and enlarge when the fitting opportunity presents itself. He who is afraid of risking a hundred dollars will certainly never become rich by his efforts.

The work of God is no exception to this same law. A liberal expenditure pays better than a niggardly one. If a church is constantly running into debt, one of two things is tolerably certain; either it is without a pastor, and is conducting its operations on the cheap principle; or if it has a pastor, it is paying him an insufficient salary. Churches, as a rule, that pay good salaries don't get into debt; while they who pay poor ones do, and they are rightly served.

In secular business, if you want to get and keep a good servant, you must pay him well, and you know it is profitable to do it. Ministers are not yet entirely angelic. They are men, and they are liable—indeed, very liable—to be influenced by human considerations, as well as Divine impluses.

As to "Systematic Giving," of which much has been heard, not much need be said here. No doubt system in all things is good. The man who gives, like the man who works, systematically, will be likely to accomplish more than the man who does not. Such is the cupidity of even sanctified human nature, that it is probably an advantage to make a liberal bargain with one's self, on behalf of the cause of God, and stick to it.

The system incidentally recognized in the New Testament is that of giving to God's cause as God has prospered us. "Upon the first day of the week let every one of you lay by him in store, as God hath prospered him, that there may be no gatherings when I come." 1 Cor. 16 ch. 2 v.

But there is a larger, if not a higher law, which it

behooves us constantly to recognize and act upon, that not merely a part, but all belongs to God. If anything belongs to Him everything does, and only that offering can be acceptable which is thorough and complete. "Ye are not your own." "Ye are Christ's." Our material possessions, our bodies, our faculties, our souls, all we are and all we have, belong, by the rights of purchase and blessing, to the Redeemer.

Is this law sufficiently recognized, and the Divine claims fully admitted? I fear not. If God were addressing the church of to-day, through some specially inspired medium, I see no reason for supposing there would be any considerable modification of His language when He spoke to His ancient people, through the mouth of the prophet: "Return unto me, and I will return unto you, saith the Lord of Hosts. But ye said: wherein shall we return? Will a man rob God? Yet ye have robbed me. But ye say, wherein have we robbed thee? In tithes and offerings. Ye are cursed with a curse, for ye have robbed me, even this whole nation. Bring ye all the tithes into the storehouse, that there may be meat in mine house, and prove me now herewith, saith the Lord of Hosts, if I will not open you the windows of heaven, and pour you out a blessing, that there shall not be room enough to receive it." Mat. 3 ch. 7-10 vs.

Do the people of God to-day admit this charge, and will they accept this ancient challenge of the Almighty? Let us do our part, and God will certainly do His. Let us furnish, and equip, and fully maintain the instrumentalities for the propagation of His Gospel, and He will give the blessing abundantly.

The needs of the world are great and ever pressing, and if we do not come to the rescue, who will? Men are perishing, even at our very doors, for lack of spiritual knowledge, and if we, who have the light and the truth, do not give unto them, who will? We are the repositories of light, and we are commanded to let the light *shine before men.* What is needed to-day, in the church of Christ the world throughout, is a fuller and a deeper consecration, and the development, on the largest possible scale, of all material and spiritual gifts, and the Spirit of God resting upon them.

CHAPTER IX.

The Pastoral Relation.

THAT the pastoral relation is an important one will be readily admitted, and like another important relationship, of great antiquity and almost universal prevalence, it should not be entered upon lightly, "but reverently, discreetly, advisedly, and in the fear of God, duly considering the objects for which it was ordained." Whether it is always, or even in the majority of cases, entered upon in the spirit here indicated may be seriously doubted. Indeed, I think, we may, with good reason, fear, that if all the pastoral relations now existing, among all denominations of Christians, were tested by that standard, and dissolved if found wanting, there would be the greatest ecclesiastical upheaval that the Church of Christ has seen for eighteen hundred years.

Perhaps you may think this statement extravagant,

and upon the first blush it probably seems so, but the more you think about it the more you will be likely to come to the conclusion, that, after all, it is no vain imagining, and no exaggeration, but rather a plain, honest forecast of the probable facts in the supposed contingency.

Who are to blame for all this, the Pastors or the churches? Both, but mainly the latter.

That there is a lack of fitness which leads to perpetual change is matter of common, every day observation. This is clearly chargeable, to a certain extent, to the ordinary methods in vogue for securing settlements. And here blame belongs to both sides—Pastor and church—and unworthy scheming is not by any means uncommon, such as would not be likely to do much credit to any respectable business concern.

A young man, just on the point of leaving college, was seeking his first pastorate. He preached with great acceptance, for several Sabbaths, to a pastorless church. The impression was very favorable, in fact, as far as he and others equally interested could see, unanimously so. A meeting was called to decide the matter of extending a call. A resolution was submitted, and passed, that a call be extended. And then, without negativing this, another resolution was passed, that he should be invited for three months only; and he was told, in the communication that was subsequently sent to him—after reciting both resolutions—that he was to inform the official, who made the communication, whether he accepted the call for three months. One would like to believe that this was downright ignorance, but probably it was not. It was more likely a deliberate attempt to thwart the will of the majority; and it succeeded, for the young aspirant for office saw through it at once, and he immediately wrote that he declined to accept.

A Pastor of fair ability, and considerable experience, was incidentally supplying the pulpit of a vacant church for a few Sabbaths. The church had recently extended a call, and it was being considered by the brother who had received it. One or two leading brethren interviewed the party of the second part, and asked him if he would be favorable to accepting a call. With surprise he asked if they had not a call to another brother pending, which they admitted. Then said he, you should wait for your answer, and see whether your call be accepted or declined, before making any overtures to me. Upon the assurance of a favorable consideration they were, evidently, prepared to set the machinery in operation for withdrawing the call at once, without waiting for an answer. Future developments showed that if they had received the necessary encouragement, and done this, they would have been excusable to a certain extent, for the brother, who received the call, was holding it in abeyance in the expectation of receiving one from a larger church, for which he was scheming and waiting, and sacrificing his Christian consistency in more ways than one. As soon, however, as he got the hint that he was running some risk of losing both, he quickly despatched his acceptance, following it, almost immediately, by himself and all his belongings.

These instances might be multiplied, but perhaps not to much advantage. It is certainly not pleasant to reflect that any who bear the Christian name, whether lay or cleric, can act so unworthily; but nothing can be gained by shutting our eyes, or denying the facts that are well known to exist.

The problem of settling a pastor is apt to be a considerable one, and I have, for a long time, had grave doubts of the wisdom of many of the methods that are employed for securing that desirable end. Of course I am speaking of those churches who have entire, or almost entire, control of the selection of their ministers. Of the others no useful result would be likely to come from any observations of mine.

They have their systems into which they have grown, and which they are likely to retain.

But there is one thing common to them all, which may be briefly referred to here, and that is, that the ministers of all denominations are dependent upon those to whom they minister for their temporal support. Now, correct as this may be, and doubtless is, in theory, it works badly, in quite a number of cases, in practice. Under such conditions fidelity is necessarily at a discount, and the fearless man of God is liable to suffer harm. For, it is a fact, that people will profess to admire fidelity in a minister, and yet quietly, but in a most effectual way, resent it, when it strikes them, or they think it strikes them, personally. In saying this I know, most assuredly, whereof I affirm.

And here, before I forget it, let me enter my most solemn and emphatic protest against a practice which is altogether too common, in churches of the purely democratic order, where there is no effectual check upon anything that is done, outside of the organization; and where, oftentimes, moral considerations which should most prevail, seem to prevail the least, in certain exigencies. "Thou shalt not steal," might be shouted, in stentorian tones, into the ears of some churches with a measure of appropriateness and effect, when they are intent, in their vaunted opulence and strength, in not only coveting, but also really pilfering the best gifts, or what they think the best gifts.

"We that are strong ought to bear the infirmities of the weak, and not to please ourselves," is not acted upon at all, but the reverse; and hence the strong are made stronger and the weak weaker. It is downright robbery, and opposed, as clearly as anything can be, to the spirit of Christ, and the plain statements and principles of the New Testament— of which the above is a sample—and yet men who call themselves Christians seem to glory in it.

I have said there are different methods of securing Pastors. So there are. The old time candidating plan is considerably in vogue yet, and may never go out of fashion altogether, but in the larger and more opulent churches it is giving place, a good deal, to what we may call the Committee Method; and a committee, in the modern ecclesiastical sense, may be composed of one person or several. This committee may be appointed by the church, or it may be self-appointed, as some of them unquestionably are. In either case it is supposed to contain the quintessence of the wisdom of that particular community. These brethren are credited, generally, with knowing all about the needs of the church, and as they have its welfare deeply at heart, they, of course, know what kind of a man is needed.

A committee of this kind varies very much in its scope and powers. It may be limited, or it may be practically unlimited. It may enquire, hear, judge, decide, and then recommend, and its recommendation may or may not be accepted by the church; or it may be understood that its recommendation, whatever it be, will be accepted, which, of course, gives it, practically, unlimited authority and power.

I am not disposed, at present, to say which is best, or even whether either is good. I have my doubts, and serious doubts, and what I do think will be better known and understood a little further on.

It is claimed for this method of securing a Pastor that it has answered admirably in many cases. So it may have, but I suppose it would not be difficult to prove that those who have adopted it have been led, in many cases, perhaps unconsciously, into grievous errors; and these are, to a large extent, necessarily incident to the method itself.

One or more of the collective wisdom may be despatched, or may despatch themselves, to hear on the sly some one whose reputation for excellence, in some respect, has been wafted on the breeze of popular applause.

The idea is that that they will be able to hear his average sermon; what he does at home, and what he is able to maintain all the year round. Besides, they can make enquiries, etc.

Do these missions always prove successful? I fear not. Are no mistakes made resulting in consequent failure and disaster to somebody? I think mistakes are frequently made, and necessarily so too. Take one or two cases in point, the verity of which you may rely on.

A was requested to go and hear B preach, and report

to C, which was the committee of a pastorless church in a large city. A, went and heard the gifted brother, all unawares of course to the brother himself, and duly sent in his report, which was to the effect that "B was a man of advanced ideas," a most indefinite and unfortunate description. It might be commendatory or otherwise, according to the construction placed upon it.

To a great many people a man of advanced ideas is a veritable scarecrow, something to awaken considerable apprehension, and make them feel uneasy; and, indeed, something to be shunned. Or, he is one who is likely to do considerable damage if let loose in any community, like the traditional bull in the traditional China shop. He is supposed to have small respect for the past, and for old worn out ideas and theories; to be exceedingly radical, and being a bold thinker there is no telling when he will bring something out of his restless brain that may come very near upsetting everything, and turning the world upside down. He is altogether therefore a dangerous character, or if not as bad as that, he is, at least, what some timid people call an impracticable man, which is nearly the same as being a dangerous one.

To some, however,—and God be praised for it—he is not all this, but something altogether different. He is simply one who has brains, and courage, and industry enough to do his own thinking, and consequently he moves, advances, is a growing man, and is liable to create a little life and movement in others, to their unspeakable benefit, and, perhaps, to their eternal advantage.

To make this veritable episode short let me say that the man of advanced ideas was never asked to show himself in that vacant pulpit, and it is safe to venture the assertion that that unfortunate, but nevertheless truthful, description, killed all his chances of ecclesiastical preferment in that direction.

Take another case. A committee representing a vacancy in "the City of Churches," went to another city of no mean importance or dimensions, to hear a pastor of some repute, and make all due enquiry concerning him, with a view of seeing whether they deemed him suitable and competent to occupy the position of pastor of the church which they represented.

What they thought of him as a preacher, when they heard him, I am not in a position to say, for the simple and all sufficient reason that I have no information upon that matter. The point I wish to make is, that in prosecuting their enquiries —so unwisely will even wise men act sometimes—they called upon the one man in the whole community, who, unfortunately for him and all concerned, was the pastor's avowed and open enemy. And it was a case of

"I do not like you Dr. Bell.
The reason why I cannot tell."

It was a very bad case, as all such cases are liable to be. No dislike—I will not say hatred—is so bitter as that which has no proper foundation, and which is alike unintelligent and unreasonable. Said He, whom no man had any just cause to hate, "they hated me *without a cause.*"

What the result of the interview was may be easily conjectured. It would be expecting too much from human nature, and denying all human experience, to prognosticate a favorable issue under the circumstances. Nothing came of the visit of the mysterious strangers as far as the Pastor was concerned, and even white robed charity will admit that possibly a grave mistake was made, and a great wrong done to some one. The Lord have mercy upon us—poor miserable sinners!

Recommendations, and testimonials to character and fitness, from men occupying distinguished positions in the church, have come to be discounted considerably in recent years, and it is believed by many with good and sufficient reason. And yet the case is not unusual, even now, when a leading man in college or church, especially if he be self-assertive and naturally dominant, will wield immense, and well nigh despotic influence, within a given domain, more or less extended. He becomes a sort of little pope, especially little; that is, if you analyze him closely you will probably find more of the little than the pope after all.

I have known such men, and I am free to confess that I have held them in great and merited contempt, and so have you. And I have known churches so transparently imbecile, and so abominably servile and foolish, as to sacrifice their own individuality, and to accept men for Pastors upon the simple fiat of such men. And also I have known these said churches refuse to look at, much less give a hearing to, men of unimpeachable character and integrity, and undoubted ability, because the said autocrat refused to nod his head in that direction. "O foolish Galatians, who hath bewitched you, that ye should not *obey the truth.*"

I am far from saying, or wishing to be understood, that all influential men are of the stamp I have feebly portrayed. I am willing to admit that men may become influential by genuine goodness and undoubted ability, and that there are such it would be unfair and ungenerous not to admit; but I must be allowed to say that, in my deliberate judgment, and as the result of considerable experience and observation, they are largely in the minority. Nor, perhaps, can it well be otherwise in this essentially wicked and stupid world that is not naturally friendly to goodness and virtue; and the same, I fear, must be confessed in regard to many churches where common sense is, unhappily, as rare as the queen of virtues—charity.

The desire to secure pastors, who have made what is called a good record, is a prevailing weakness of many churches at the present day. Ask them what they mean by a pastor who has made a good record, and you will find they do not mean one eminent for piety, goodness, fidelity, purity, consecration, and other common, but priceless virtues; but they mean a man who has made a great noise, and achieved some notable success; without enquiring, very particularly, into the nature and reality of the success, or the means by which it has been accomplished. They want, and they mean to have, a man who has been a decided success somewhere, as they understand success, in the hope, of course, that his great abilities, or something else, will achieve results as great and notable for them.

I say this is not uncommon, and it is thought by many to be a right and praiseworthy ambition. I dissent from this entirely, and without any hesitation am prepared to affirm and maintain that it is wrong in principle, utterly delusive, oftentimes greatly disappointing, and even, in some cases, disastrous to all concerned.

God does not judge his servants by what we call success. The rewards of the future will not be apportioned upon that basis, but upon an entirely different one, namely fidelity; and it is neither right nor safe for the church of Christ to depart from the Divine standard. Besides it is essentially a worldly principle, and a worldly spirit. It is regulating a sacred function, and a religious institution, by secular policy and wisdom.

It is delusive too, for we are poor judges of what success is. We are very liable to make great and grievous mistakes. The record is not always faultless; not always to be implicitly depended upon Sad as it is, let it be known, and not readily forgotten, that as a rule —whatever the exceptions may be—it is the untrustworthy schemer, and not the honest worker, that makes the record that tells in statistics, and in religious papers and periodicals, and upon which many rely who think they are more than ordinarily wise.

And then, be it observed, that when success is not largely fictitious, or merely apparent, but real and substantial, it does not follow that the same or similar results will be accomplished in another sphere by the same worker. And it is just here that mistakes are made that lead to disappointment and possible disaster. The very qualities that ensure a Pastor's eminent success in one sphere, far from making probable his success in another, may lead to his comparative if not utter failure; because there may not be the same fitness, and the aptitudes and conditions are not unlikely to be altogether different; and upon fitness and harmony of conditions peace and prosperity much depend.

This is not an exceptional contingency we are considering, but one of constant occurrence, and one which many Pastors and churches have recognized with lasting regret when too late to remedy. So that we practically come to this, that in the majority of cases at least, if not all, it would be safer and wiser not to adopt the record theory as a guide to action, and thus escape the temptations to covetousness and stealing. Leave the useful and successful minister alone. If he is really doing an important work, with more than average adaptation and success, that is an all-sufficient reason for his remaining where he is; and no church that cares to be accounted strictly honest, or that is really wise, will make any effort to tempt him away. If, however, on the other hand, the usefulness and the success are largely fictitious, and therefore of the nature of a fraudulent pretence to bolster up a reputation upon which to base a bid for a rise, you have made a lucky escape, and may hope to retain the sweet consciousness that "honesty is the best policy."

Having offered these free criticisms upon some of the prevailing methods for facilitating pastoral settlements, I may be expected, and that not unreasonably, to offer some suggestions as to the best and wisest course for a church to pursue in that periodically recurring exigency called a vacancy.

And here let me observe, at the outset, that the first thing to be done is to get rid of the idea, so deeply set and so prevalent, that a Pastor is absolutely necessary to the usefulness and prosperity of a church. I say absolutely necessary, for that is the ground generally and practically taken. I am far from meaning that a Pastor is unnecessary, or that a church may be as useful and prosperous without one as with. But I do mean that a church properly constituted, and that has been well instructed and trained, may and ought to maintain its well-being and usefulness practically unimpaired without a Pastor; and until such time as, unmistakably, the right man makes his appearance.

It is somewhat amusing to call to mind some of the stock phrases that have crept into use to describe a church that is temporarily without a pastor. It is a vacant church, a destitute church, a church in a destitute condition, etc. Some prolific scribe who contributes to the news column of the denominational organ, or writes the annual letter to sister churches, will say: "As a church we are destitute," and instantly every one knows precisely what is meant; and it may be known to some that that same brother has been the main instrument in causing that destitution which he so pathetically describes, and seems so sincerely to mourn.

And then a church is sometimes spoken of, in equally plaintive tone and language, as a flock without a shepherd— meaning, of course, an under-shepherd—and yet this poor shepherdless flock may have, right in the midst of it, one or two able-bodied shepherds ; but the sheep have long since ceased to hear their voice, and prefer the voice of a stranger.

These cases are not uncommon, and when they occur they reflect no credit upon either the Christianity or the wisdom of the churches concerned.

I will venture to suggest that the next thing to be done is to adopt the best means, that are possible and available, for the regular and efficient supply of the pulpit. And I do not mean the supply of the pulpit with the one prevailing and absorbing idea of securing a Pastor, but simply with the view of making that important branch of the church's work as useful and effective as possible in the inevitable interim. That is the one imperative duty to attend to, and it should have all the thought, and care, and time, and intelligent performance which its paramount importance merits. The very best talent that is available should be got, and remunerated as liberally as the resources of the church will allow.

I would not ask any one to preach on trial, or with a view to a call, or as one brother very innocently, but aptly put it, to be *sampled*. He was referring to a certain period in the history of a church, and to make his meaning, as to time, plain, he said it was when there was a vacancy, and they were engaged in sampling ministers. I had never heard that particular descriptive phrase before, and as it somewhat interested and amused me, it stuck, and has lingered in my memory ever since.

There are two objections to this sampling process. The first is that it is not very dignified, and proper dignity in this transaction should count for something. The second is that the best men are not liable to produce a very good specimen of what they can do, in an ordinary way, when they know they are being sampled; and especially when the samplers are known to be so different in their capacity, education and disposition; and many, perhaps, not very competent to form any reliable judgment at all.

Throw the sampling to the winds, and fill the pulpit, from Sabbath to Sabbath, with the very best talent that can be got, and the problem of settling a Pastor will eventually solve itself; and I believe in a more satisfactory manner than by many of the methods that are ordinarily employed to expedite that desirable end. Let a church work faithfully, act wisely, wait patiently, and the right man will, in due time, appear, and will not fail to be recognized. Many churches have had to mourn undue precipitancy, but few, if any, have had to regret making haste slowly.

What are the advantages to be derived from following out the course here suggested? Several. Less mistakes will likely be made; more lasting settlements will be effected; the church will become more self-reliant; and its expectations, in regard to the Pastor, more moderate, and its demands less exacting; and this is certainly a movement in the right direction.

When a church has successfully solved the problem of obtaining a pastor, the next one that waits for solution is how to retain him.

A good and efficient pastor is not only a valuable acquisition, but he is worth making some effort to keep. I do not know that anything can be offered in the way of suggestion here, beyond what is obvious and common place, but even that may have some practical value as contributing, in some measure, to the sum total of truth in regard to an important relation, which cannot but affect for good or evil the character and destiny of many. Take a few suggestions :

1. The pastor should have the entire confidence of his people, for without that he is like Samson shorn of his locks, and weakness and instability must ensue. He should not only have it, but he should *know* that he has it, else it is nearly worthless. The knowledge of the fact will create in him a feeling of content and satisfaction; and it will brace his mind, encourage his heart, and nerve his soul to do the best that is in him.

This confidence should be made abundantly apparent by deeds not words. Words are cheap, proverbially so; a cent a bushel would be quite a price for some of them. Deeds cost something, perhaps more than money, and thereby is their genuine worth attested. "My little children, let us not love in word, neither in tongue, but in deed and in truth." 1 John, 3 ch. 18 v.

Of course in making these observations, I am assuming that the Pastor is a man who is worthy of confidence, and *transparently so;* and I mean by that, that it is so apparent that you are not left in any doubt about it; neither do you have to look long and earnestly to find it out. I assume also that his demeanor and conduct are such as to merit, without any faltering, its retention. If, however, upon fair and trustworthy grounds of observation, it is evident these are lacking, confidence not only may, but should be withdrawn, and the sooner the better, so that the worthy may be protected, and the unworthy meet their just reward.

2. The second requisite for retaining a Pastor is to give him cause to believe that his people have formed a fairly just estimate of his worth and capabilities, so that he will not be liable to be either over-rated or under-rated. There is one thing that unthinking people don't seem to realize, and that is, that their dear Pastor—as in their gushing tenderness they sometimes call him—can be as effectually injured by the over-estimate, and extravagant eulogies and compliments of his well meaning friends, as by the reverse, proceeding from those whose judgment and attitude are different.

Many a good man has wished, most heartily and sincerely, and with just cause, to be delivered from his friends; for if he is a man of genuine ability, he will be likely to form a moderate estimate of himself; and whatever clashes with that may come as a surprise, if not a pain; and that sweet unconsciousness of the genuine man, which is so charming and so rare, will be disturbed. Besides, exaggerated estimates, and extravagant eulogies, lead to possible disaster by creating unreasonable expectations which can never be realized, and which therefore are likely to end in disappointment.

But some, and perhaps many, think that the strongest tendency is in the opposite direction, that of underrating a pastor. I can only say that neither my experience nor my observation confirms this view. But where it does exist, as it certainly does in some cases, it is both discouraging and injurious, alike to the pastor and his charge, for both suffer together inevitably.

As a matter of fact truth cannot be sacrificed either way without possible, and perhaps lasting, injury to all concerned. No genuine man, and true hearted minister, wishes to pass for more than he is, nor less; and only such is worth making any effort to keep. All else is chaff which let the wind drive away.

3. The third requisite for retaining a pastor is that of giving him an adequate temporal support; and such a

support as will be a fair and respectable embodiment of the financial ability of his charge. And I wish it to be understood that it should be adequate not only so far as his present and immediate daily needs are concerned, but it should meet the contingencies of life; and especially that supremest, and most common, and most imperative of all contingencies, when he may, perhaps for many years, outlive his vigor and his usefulness.

What an adequate support is may be an open question generally considered. One thousand dollars per annum, or less, may be adequate in one place; and yet two thousand may be only respectable poverty in another. It is also true that the ministry, like other ranks of life, furnishes examples of sad mis-management and extravagance where no amount of salary avails to keep out of debt. But these cases we may hope and believe are rare, and we know the *chances* of a reckless expenditure are very exceptional. Seldom is a Pastor's income much of a temptation in that direction, but rather the reverse. Of one thing I am sure that if you want the best that a Pastor can do, and wish him to labor on with average contentment and real vigor, you must contrive to make his mind easy in regard to his financial condition, and outlook. Treat him liberally, and he will be more likely to have his affections fixed upon where he is, and what he has to do, and less upon some other possible place where he is not. In other words, make his position worth keeping, and worth laboring to keep, —for remember he is human as you are—and wishes to meet the world honestly as you do.

4. A church should seek to cultivate the grace of being considerate, and contrive to be reasonable and moderate in its demands for service. "Thou shalt not kill," is still in force, and is as applicable to the individual church as the individual man. A man can be done to death by over-work and anxiety as well as by slow poison ; and severe as the statement may seem, I fear the church of Christ is not altogether guiltless in this respect. God only, absolutely, knows, and where there is blood He will surely make inquisition for it.

It is believed by some people, and not without reason, that of all corporate bodies, that are said to be without souls, a church can, in certain moods and circumstances, be the most thoughtless, the most exacting, and even the most cruel. It is certainly amazing with what complacency, or at least indifference, professing Christians will look on while a pastor is visibly working himself into the grave, and not utter a word of friendly and intelligent remonstrance, or lend a helping hand to avert, what must be a calamity to some, and perhaps to many, the possible premature extinction of a useful life.

And in saying this I am far from wishing to convey the impression that all pastors are over-worked. There are some who, no doubt, have the "pleasant places," and the "goodly heritage;" but these do not fall to the many, and not always to the most worthy.

Neither do I think it can be successfully maintained that ministers, as a class, work harder for a living—looking at their calling in that light—than men in other walks of life. Indeed, I suppose the general opinion is that they have a very much easier time than other people. Neither extreme is correct. The ministry is a laborious calling when the duties are faithfully performed, but not more so than many others; and perhaps the average remuneration is not less; but I think any unprejudiced observer, who is competent to judge, will admit that it is more liable to unreasonable expectations and demands; and it is just here where the burden comes that leads to a temporary break-down, or an utter collapse of the powers of endurance and effective work.

When this happens, as happen it does with moderate frequency, the Christianity of the church is put to the test.

The test, in many cases, is met nobly and well. In others, to the eternal disgrace of those concerned, it is not; and the disabled Pastor is cast off, and left to shift for himself, and solve the problem of physical regenerration unaided and alone. Am I severe? I am not, or if I am, know thou who readest these lines that it is the severity of truth; and if the mantle of shame cometh to thy cheek so let it be. For me it is enough that "I speak that I do know, and testify that I have seen."

5. As a final, and somewhat practical, suggestion, let me remark that if you wish to retain your Pastor, and keep him in good health and strength for the effective performance of his duties, you should give him an annual vacation; and insist, most strenuously, upon his taking it, and using it in such a way as to best secure the end sought, namely, his physical and mental recuperation.

Of one thing I am as sure as I can be of any truth,

that any worker, especially a brain worker, and most especially a ministerial brain worker, can do more effective work in eleven months than he can in twelve; that is, if he use the twelfth wisely, and for the object above indicated. Many a good man has mourned in secret, and felt grieved at heart over the want of thought or the illiberality of his people in this particular. He feels the need, but he will not beg, and he may not wish, for proper reasons, to boldly prefer a claim. It should not be necessary. Selfishness, if no higher motive, should prompt the church not to permit but to insist upon a needed change and rest. The bow must be unbent, for a season, or it will not abide in strength, nor shoot the arrow of truth with unerring aim.

He has, strictly speaking, no Sabbath. The day of rest for all mankind is to him a day of exhausting toil, and this continues the year throughout. Neither can he successfully make a Sabbath, for whatever his plans in this respect may be, they are liable to daily and hourly frustration. So much the more necessary that he should have, without fail and without grudging, an annual Sabbath. So let it be, and with a free hand, and a willing heart; and the fruit and blessing will be sure and manifold.

Of course, if some ingenuously enquiring brother is anxious to know how most effectually to get rid of a Pastor—having perhaps some benevolent scheme of that kind as a not remote possibility—I can only say, do, and get as many of the dear people as possible to do just the opposite of what has been advised with the view of retaining him. Withdraw your confidence and take special pains to let him know it. Persuade yourself into an incorrect and unjust estimate of his worth and capabilities, for that will create an atmosphere about you which his moral sensibilities will not fail to detect. See that his salary develops in the inverse ratio of his needs, for it will tend to make him humble, and show him most conclusively and convincingly that he should not trust in man, nor expect the adequate rewards of his labor here. Be as inconsiderate, unreasonable, and exacting as possible. Don't let him have any vacation. Keep him grinding out sermons all the time, or if he slip away for a Sabbath or two without leave let him understand that you don't like it, and that he had better not repeat the experiment. Keep this up, faithfully and persistently, and get as many as you can to join in the hunt, and the chances are that the dear Pastor will ere long find another sphere, if not here, then in the Great Hereafter.

If you ask my advice about attempting any or all of the above, I say—Don't.

"Touch not mine anointed, and do my prophets no harm."

CHAPTER X.

The Ethics of Christianity.

WHAT about them? This much, at least for the present, that they have come to be very much neglected; in fact, for the matter of that, literally snowed under that sum total of revivalistic theology, "only believe."

"Only believe," and then do what you like. "Only believe," and then live a selfish, grasping, worldly life." "Only believe," and then be as unscrupulous as your neighbors. "Only believe," and yet keep on acting the Devil, and doing the Devil's work. "Only believe," and then heaven will be opened to you some day, after you have got all you can out of this world ; thus, making the best of both worlds. Substantially and practically, that is the theology of a great many so-called Christians at the present day, and anything more odious or pernicious could scarcely be.

It makes Christianity a by-word and a reproach among men. It comes near, very near, making even the faithful stumble. It evokes the laughter of fiends and the tears of angels. It is the great stumbling-block to the onward march of truth. Christ is wounded in the house of his friends, or professed friends; for enemies of the worst kind they certainly are.

Does this language seem extravagant? If so, be it so. Alas! for once at least, it is the extravagance of simple truth. What is here put down, in language not otherwise carefully selected, except with the view of presenting a condition of things known to exist—in all its naked deformity and repulsiveness—is secretly acknowledged by many who have not the courage of their convictions, and who do not reprove and expose it as they should. Alas! for the watchmen on the walls, for a fearful day of reckoning is surely at hand.

I am neither an alarmist nor a fanatic because I put forth these sentiments without circumlocution or reservation. "I am not mad, most noble Festus, but speak forth the words of truth and soberness." I am simply giving utterance to—proclaiming upon the housetop—the unspoken convictions of hundreds and thousands, who have eyes to see, ears to hear, and understanding to understand, but who will not or cannot command their tongues to speak the thought that is in them. Small thanks, I suppose, I shall get for pushing a crusade along this line, but as I don't happen to be in quest of thanks, I shall not be likely to meet with a very severe disappointment.

Let me explain what I mean by the ethics of Christianity. As ethics and morals are synonymous, and morals relate to character and conduct, therefore the ethics of Christianity are related to and comprised in the Christian life.. They are the legitimate and inevitable fruits of a belief in the Christ of God. Faith in a Divine person must, as a necessary result, produce a Divine life, or a life approximating to the Divine pattern, just as certainly as effect follows cause. "Faith without works is dead," and dead faith is no faith at all, for faith is a living thing. It has life in it, and is necessarily active and productive. Simple, and self-evident, as this truth is, there is abundant and constant need for its being emphasized, even at the risk of being charged with preaching, what some people call a gospel of works.

And, truly, there is a gospel of works, and he must be blind indeed who fails to see it. It is the outcome and final analysis, and that by which each must stand to be judged, and by which, in his deeper consciousness, he must constantly judge himself. Need I remind you of the twenty-fifth chapter of Matthew, that marvellous indictment, and masterly summing up and application of all that Christ said on earth. It runs along the line of works pure and simple. We are given clearly to understand, in words that no man need mistake, that whatever the grounds of present connection and acceptance may be, the ultimate analysis and judgment, which will decide the complexion and condition of the future for each one, will be upon the basis of what has been done, or not done. "Inasmuch as ye have done it unto one of the least of these my brethren, ye have done it unto me. . . . . . . Inasmuch as ye did it not to one of the least of these ye did it not to me. . . . . And these shall go away unto everlasting punishment—but the righteous into life eternal."

Thus, the tree—the human tree I mean—will be judged not by the roots, nor by the trunk, nor by the branches, nor by the leaves, and not even by the bloom it may put forth, but by the fruit it bears. For heaven's sake, and your own, don't mistake this thing; and don't forget that it is further said upon authority which cannot be called in question—indeed, the same authority—that "they that have done good shall come forth unto the resurrection of life, and they that have done evil unto the resurrection of damnation."

You say you are saved. So be it; but did you ever sit down and calmly push thought and reflection far enough to find out and realize to yourself what is really meant by that important statement? Did you ever think that possibly your life—your every-day life—may be giving the lie to it. It is not necessary for your life to be a grossly sinful one to do that. It may be outwardly decorous and correct, and more or less devout and sincere—that is, devout and sincere on special occasions—and yet it may fall so utterly and so constantly below the Christ-life, in its general tenor and level, as to place in doubt, or discredit your pretensions altogether.

Again you say you are saved. By whom? from what? and how? These are three important questions you should be able to answer intelligently and satisfactorily.

By whom? You say by Jesus Christ. That is satisfactory, and all that need be said.

From what? From sin you say. Right you are again, but be kind enough to yourself to try and take in the full and literal significance of what you are saying. Take the Apostle's definition, for it will help you much. "But now being made free from sin, and become servants to God, ye have your fruit unto holiness, and the end everlasting life." How that word fruit comes in, and the kind of fruit, "fruit unto holiness," and this precedes and culminates in everlasting life.

You, like many others, as you unfortunately have been taught, are thinking of and looking forward to everlasting life as something absolutely secured, on a sort of commercial basis, forgetting all the while the vital connection between it and the fruit unto holiness. You must not separate these two, for God hath joined them together. Moreover, how can you say that you are saved from sin when it is clearly apparent that it is constantly, and perhaps increasingly, asserting its dominion over you. It is not perceptible to others that you are daily growing into the likeness of Christ, who knew no sin, but may be the reverse. You have clearly and manifestly made a mistake here, perhaps for the want of a clear-cut definition to begin with.

You, perhaps, think that being saved *in* sin is the same as being saved *from* sin, but it is not so. Sin and its consequences, although as closely allied as cause and effect can make them, are different, very different; and anyone who will think seriously for a moment will see it. And you fondly and delusively imagine that because, by a certain arrangement to which you say you have given your personal acquiescence, you are delivered from the latter you are therefore from the former. The fact is, you may be, or you may not be; but your character and life—what you are and what you do—must be the proof, and the only proof available in the case. It is a question of fact, and must be tested by experience and not testimony.

This is simply rising to the level of what a Christian should and must be, even upon the basis of the first principles of the gospel of Christ; and the sooner the church comes to realize, and act upon the realization, that the testimony of the life, and not that of the lips, is the true revelation and test of Christian character and standing, the better it will be for the church and for all concerned.

It is a fact worthy of note—for in theological discussion it is not unfrequently overlooked—that the consequences of sin follow inevitably, so that there is no actual deliverance from them, at least in this life. The law of God cannot be broken with impunity by either saint or sinner, saved or unsaved. It is ceaseless in its operation, and absolutely inexorable, and is no respecter of persons; for the broken law exacts its penalty from all, and never fails. Indeed, from the nature of things it cannot fail, any more than God can.

This consideration has weighed heavily upon the minds of some people, and has raised what seemed to them a formidable difficulty in regard to the gospel scheme, which finds expression in the question: If Christ suffered for sin—universal sin, the sin of all men—why do we suffer? This difficulty, formidable as it may seem at first sight, instantly diappears when we remember that Christ died for sin, died to save men from sin, and not to free them from the natural and inevitable operation of law.

The infraction of law has from all eternity, and will to all eternity carry with it its appropriate penalty. "Whatsoever a man soweth *that* shall he also reap." There is no escape from that, either in this world or the next. That is, and must be, a universal and endless law of being.

So that instead of the glory of what Christ has done, being, in anywise or to any extent, obscured by the foregoing consideration, it is thrown into stronger relief, and becomes more manifest; and what we may be permitted to call the ethical value is more clearly seen. Christ lived and died to put away sin. He dealt with the primal cause of all evil. He didn't lop off the branches, but struck at the root of the tree. He went down to the foundation and source of all the sorrow and wickedness of the world. He dealt with the cause, and through that with the effects. "Behold! the Lamb of God which taketh away the sin of the world." "Thou shalt call his name Jesus for he shall save his people from their sins." "He was manifested to take away our sins." "He is the propitiation for our sins; and not for ours only, but also for the whole world." "Christ died for our sins according to the Scriptures." "He hath made him to be sin for us." "He appeared to put away sin by the sacrifice of himself." "Christ was once offered to bear the sins of many."

It surely must be evident to the dullest understanding what the meaning of these scriptures is. It is so plain. Christ died for sin, to put away sin, to save men from sin, to conquer sin, to kill sin ; and when believers in Him rise to the level of desiring to be freed from sin rather than from its consequences, as a primary consideration, we may expect a higher type of Christian and of Christianity. We do not deem him to repent after a Godly sort who is simply sorry because of the evil effects that come upon him as the result of his transgressions ; neither should we regard him as believing after a Godly sort who aims at escaping the penalty of sin rather than sin itself.

The whole end and aim of faith in Christ should be not escaping pains and penalties, present or future, but escaping sin, and becoming daily more like Him, the sinless One.

The third question we noted waits for an answer. How are you saved? You say, of course, by believing in Jesus Christ. Right you are again. The answer is unquestionably correct, because it is undoubtedly scriptural ; and yet how stereotyped and comparatively meaningless, in a great many cases, that answer has become. How much it does mean, and yet alas! how little it imports in the average grade of testimony. It is as deep as hell and as high as heaven—for it is the link of power that saves from the one and exalts to the other —and yet not unfrequently it is practically reduced to the meagre dimensions of the assent of the understanding to a recognized plan; nay, it is sometimes not even that, being only a meaningless, and, for the most part, unintelligent repetition of a cold formula of words.

Do these strictures seem severe? It is the severity of truth, and truth even when most severe is kind. Almost anything is better than delusion, for scarcely anything is more perilous, especially in things pertaining to the welfare of the soul. Without losing sight—or wishing to lose sight —of the vicariousness of Christ's sacrifice, and the doctrine of substitution founded thereupon, it may be seriously, if not absolutely questioned, whether the faith that does not transform the life can save the soul. The faith that justifies also sanctifies. The celebrated and oft quoted text, "The just shall live by faith," means more than justification, though that is the ordinary accepted meaning. In fact. it is doubtful whether that is its primary meaning at all. But even supposing it means that, it means more, vastly more. It means that, by faith, the life of the just, or the justified one, is regulated, sanctified, ennobled, and made fruitful unto God; and where the latter is not clearly manifest the existence of the former may be regarded as exceedingly doubtful.

Fortunately the New Testament does not leave us in doubt as to the evidences, effects, and duties of the life of faith. " How shall we that are dead to sin live any longer therein." " Reckon ye also yourselves to be dead indeed unto sin, but alive unto God through Jesus Christ our Lord." " Let not sin therefore reign in your mortal body." " For sin shall not have dominion over you." " Servants to righteousness unto holiness." " Being made free from sin, and become servants to God, ye have your fruit unto holiness, and the end everlasting life." " We should bring forth fruit unto God." " There is, therefore, now no condemnation to them which are in Christ Jesus, who walk not after the flesh but after the Spirit." " Be not conformed to this world, but be ye transformed by the renewing of your mind." " Abhor that which is evil; cleave to that which is good." " Let us therefore cast off the works of darkness, and let us put on the armour of light.'

"Let us walk honestly as in the day." "The temple of God is holy, which temple ye are." "The body is not for fornication, but for the Lord, and the Lord for the body." "Ye cannot drink the cup of the Lord, and the cup of devils; ye cannot be partakers of the Lord's table, and of the table of devils." "Let us cleanse ourselves from all filthiness of the flesh and spirit, perfecting holiness in the fear of God." "That we should be holy and without blame before him in love." "That ye put off concerning the former conversation the old man, and that ye put on the new man, which after God is created in righteousness and true holiness." "That ye may be blameless and harmless, the sons of God, without rebuke, in the midst of a crooked and perverse nation, among whom ye shine as lights in the world." "Walk worthy of God who hath called you unto his kingdom and glory." "Follow after righteousness, Godliness, faith, love, patience, meekness." "Let every one that nameth the name of Christ depart from iniquity." "As obedient children, not fashioning yourselves according to the former lusts in your ignorance; but as he which hath called you is holy, so be ye holy in all manner of conversation; because it is written, be ye holy, for I am holy." "We being dead to sins, should live unto righteousness." "What manner of persons ought ye to be in all holy conversation and Godliness." "Whosoever doeth not righteousness is not of God, neither he that loveth not his brother." "For whatsoever is born of God overcometh the world; and this is the victory that overcometh the world, even our faith." "He that doeth good is of God, but he that doeth evil hath not seen God." "Who is he that overcometh the world, but he that believeth that Jesus is the Son of God." "Let your light so shine before men, that they may see your good works, and glorify your Father which is in heaven." "Not every one that saith unto me, Lord, Lord, shall enter into the kingdom of heaven, but he that doeth the will of my Father which is in heaven." "Whosoever heareth these sayings of mine and doeth them, I will liken him unto a wise man which built his house upon a rock." "He that abideth in me, and I in Him, the same bringeth forth much fruit." "Herein is my Father glorified, that ye bear much fruit, so shall ye be my disciples." "By their fruits ye shall know them." "If a man love me he will keep my words." "Ye are my friends if ye do whatsoever I command you." "In every nation he that feareth Him, and worketh righteousness, is accepted with Him." "Glory, honor, and peace, to every man that worketh good, to the Jew first, and also to the Gentile." "To whom ye yield yourselves servants to obey, his servants ye are to whom ye obey; whether of sin unto death, or of obedience unto righteousness." "We are his workmanship, created in Christ Jesus unto good works, which God hath before ordained that he should walk in them." "That He might redeem us from all iniquity, and purify unto Himself a peculiar people, zealous of good works." "This is a faithful saying, and these things I will that thou affirm constantly, that they which have believed in God might be careful to maintain good works." "What doth it profit, my brethren, though a man say he hath faith, and have not works; can (such) faith save him? Yea, a man may say, thou hast faith and I have works; shew me thy faith without thy works, and I will shew thee my faith by my works. For as the body without the spirit is dead, so faith without works is dead also." "Hereby we do know that we know Him, if we keep His commandments. He that saith I know Him, and keepeth not his commandments, is a liar, and the truth is not in him.

But whoso keepeth His word, in him verily is the love of God perfected; hereby know we that we are in Him. He that saith he abideth in Him, ought himself also so to walk, even as He walked."

I need scarcely remind you that the last two, of this somewhat long list of New Testament quotations, are from James and John. How explicit and decisive their statements are. Query whether they would not, if they were here, make a good team to head a much needed propaganda upon the basis of this truly apostolic theology.

But taking the quotations as a whole—representing as they do the very marrow and substance of all that the Divine has given us upon this subject, for our instruction and admonition—can any one fail to see that holiness, obedience, and fruitfulness flow inevitably from faith in Christ; and that where these are absent a bastard faith is being cherished; a faith which is nothing more than the mere assent of the understanding, and not the living faith which is "the gift of God," and is born of the Spirit of God.

Two agencies, totally dissimilar, and as wide as the poles in their methods, have contributed, in no inconsiderable degree, to dim the lustre of the Christian name, and hinder the growth of a healthy and fruitful Christian life—Churchism and Revivalism. One has practically, though perhaps not intentionally, taught that the church and its ordinances are all sufficient; the other with equal practicality, though probably void of the intent, has produced a wide-spread impression that an undeveloped faith in Christ is all that God requires, or the soul needs.

There need not be any doubt in the mind of the intelligent reader—who is noting carefully what is here put down—in what sense the word churchism is used in this connection; neither will he fail to see, upon a moment's reflection, that it has a somewhat widely extended application. This peculiar ism is not confined to any one particular church or denomination, although it may be more manifest in some than in others. All have it, more or less, consciously or unconsciously, though not in an equal degree; and it comes out in, what may be called, a sort of deification of the ecclesiastical organism, and the attachment of undue importance to what is merely the ceremonial expression of its life

Indeed, it is wonderful, in this wondrous age of progress in almost every department of life, that there should be such clinging to the mere paraphernalia of worship and organized Christianity. It is more than standing still ; it is going back.

Progress is in the direction of simplicity, and an insistence upon, and cultivation of, the vitalities and the essentials. Semblances are nothing, or next to nothing; truth and life, and what follows upon their development, everything.

But the evil goes deeper than this. It seems to be invested, as if by some subtle and malign power, with a fatal and self-propagating tendency downwards. Not only does this wide-spread indulgence in, and cultivation of, semblances lead to mistaking them for realities, but ultimately they come to be accepted as such ; and all the more delusively and fatally, because, perhaps, unconsciously. The stone is taken for bread, and the serpent for a fish.

Any one who will take the trouble to examine carefully, cannot fail to see, that much of what Christ charged against the church in His time, is, to a considerable extent, applicable, in varying degrees, to the church to-day ; showing that human nature, even in its professedly best forms, has the same degenerating tendencies and weakness, in all times and places.

As an example of what is here meant take the following: " But whereunto shall I liken this generation ? It is like unto children sitting in the markets, and calling unto their fellows ; and saying, we have piped unto you, and ye have not danced ; we have mourned unto you, and ye have not lamented." Matt. 11 ch. 16-17 vs.

I am quite aware that in quoting this passage, in this connection, I am departing from the ordinary accepted explanation of what must be acknowledged to be a somewhat obscure reference. The fact is, the ordinary recognized expositors don't seem to know precisely what it means, hence the great variety of conjecture and explanation. My impression is that Christ had a deeper meaning than any usually conjectured, and one accordant with common sense, and in harmony with many of His other trenchant utterances concerning that generation ; namely, that He meant to charge that professedly pious and eminently religious people with simply *playing at religion ;* a state of things which, by the way, is not uncommon at the present day.

As a sample of those trenchant utterances above referred to as harmonizing with this view, take the following : " Woe unto you Scribes and Pharisees, hyprocrites ! for ye pay tithe of mint, and anise, and cummin, and have omitted the weightier matters of the law ; judgment, mercy and faith ; these ought ye to have done, and not to leave the other undone. Ye blind guides, which strain at a gnat, and swallow a camel." Matt., 23 ch., 23-24 vs.

Perhaps some super-refined Christian, or one claiming to be such, may ask : Would you take away entirely the esthetic element in religion ? Much depends upon your ideas of the esthetic, and what you precisely mean. If you mean what the word really imports, as applied to Christianity, my answer is no. The esthetic has to do with matters of superlative beauty, and of pure taste ; and therefore Christian estheticism—if you will kindly allow the phrase—is appropriately expressed and defined thus : " Pure religion and undefiled before God and the Father is this, to visit the fatherless and the widows in their affliction, and to keep himself unspotted from the world " James, 1 ch., 27 v. That means, be good, and do good, which should be, and is, the highest ideal of man. Can there be anything more beautiful, or in better taste, than love and purity; a heart overflowing with practical sympathy for God's afflicted ones, and a soul white and clean, free from the defilement of the world?

Ah! but you say, that is not what I meant by esthetic. No, my friend, I know it is not what you meant. You meant something altogether different, not quite so high and pure as that, and therefore you are one of those to whom the scorching words, already quoted, may apply: "Ye pay tithe of mint, and anise, and cummin, and have omitted the weightier matters of the law—judgment, mercy, and faith."

Possibly, and even probably, the most injurious manifestation of churchism, from which the present generation of Christians is not by any means free, is that which shows itself in the pride and selfishness of the individual church, and in denominational arrogance and exclusiveness. There is nothing more pitiable, and scarcely anything more discreditable to the Christian name. It is an offence alike to common sense, to humanity, and to the Lord of all. It is essentially a worldly spirit, and therefore utterly at variance with the spirit of Christ, and all He said and did on earth; as well as being opposed to the most solemn and repeated admonitions to individual believers and churches contained in the epistles: " Let nothing be done through strife or vain glory; but in lowliness of mind let each esteem other better than themselves." Phil. 2 ch. 3 v. Whenever I hear a member of any particular church or denomination, however high he may be ecclesiastically, vaunting the pre-eminence, and the distinguished excellence and success of the communion to which he belongs, I pity him with all sincerity, for I know he has much to unlearn and much to learn, and may be much to suffer in heavenly discipline, before he can attain the sweet temper, and rise to the simple level of the Christ-life. One only is paramount, and He says: " Learn of me, for I am *meek and lowly* in heart." " One is your Master, even Christ, and *all ye are brethren.*"

I have many times asked myself the question, How is it that so many believers in Christ utterly belie His spirit, and not only fall short of His meekness and gentleness, and His simple and pure life, but exhibit characteristics that are the very opposite, and not in a mild, but in an intense degree? I confess I have sought long and earnestly, looked over and under, and all round, for an answer that will not seem harsh and uncharitable, but in vain.

Truth which is immutable and eternal, and keeps on its majestic way in spite of us, demands that the answer shall be, that there are many professed believers who are not believers at all. They are deceiving themselves, for "if any man have not the Spirit of Christ he is none of His."

I once heard a very earnest and godly man expound this text, and he contended — very sincerely no doubt, but I think erroneously—that the spirit there means the Holy Spirit. I confess, I prefer the meaning that lies upon the surface, and that the words so plainly convey. But even supposing the Holy Spirit is meant, we reach the same conclusion, not with diminished, but added force; for "the fruit of the spirit is love, joy, peace, long suffering, gentleness, goodness, faith, meekness, temperance"—certainly the very spirit of Christ. So, it is a delusion, of the worst and most fatal kind, to cherish the thought that you believe in Christ, and are born of the spirit, if your life does not bear the fruit here indicated. You might as well affirm that a cause can exist and operate without producing its appropriate effect.

Before proceeding to offer any criticisms upon Modern Revivalism, in its relation to Christian ethics, let me carefully re-state the position I have taken, so as to guard against any misapprehension of my meaning in regard to so important a subject. I say, Revivalism as it is ordinarily conducted—whatever the exceptions may be, and there doubtless are exceptions—has tended, in no inconsiderable degree, to dim the lustre of the Christian name, and hinder the growth of a healthy Christian life; and that by producing a widespread impression that an undeveloped faith in Christ is all that God requires, or the soul needs.

And be it observed that reference is here made not alone to the efforts of professional Revivalists,—that is, men who are consecrated wholly to this kind of work—but also to the periodic efforts which occur in the individual church, with or without extraneous, supplemental aid, and which generally come about at certain seasons of the year, which are supposed to be most favorable for originating, and carrying forward to a successful issue, a special work of grace.

These special efforts are, in some sections of country and among certain classes of Christians, called "protracted meetings," and they are not inappropriately named; and the truly herculean efforts that are sometimes made "to get up an interest," indicate that there is considerable dependence upon the human; and that, possibly, vocalized force, and emotional effervescence are being mistaken for divine impulsion.

Another phase of revivalism is that of the earnest and enterprising pastor, whom you meet with here and there, who is determined, for some reason best known to himself and to God, to have his church in a state of constant revival. He thinks *that* should be the normal condition of the church, and perhaps it should if it be real, for then only will the results achieved stand the grinding tests of time and circumstance. All depends upon reality, and reality depends upon submission to Divine conditions and conformity to Divine methods.

It must be confessed, however,—and I do it with deep sorrow—that instances of these enterprising brethren, who seek to maintain a state of perpetual revival, or what passes for such, have come within the sphere of my observation, where the methods adopted, and the motives that shone through them, have been so transparently and excessively human that scarcely any stretch of charity could associate them with the Divine. In such cases it is clear, even to a mind of ordinary acuteness, that numerical success, or the reputation of being successful,—that God whom so many ignorantly worship—is looked upon as the one thing most to be desired, and by all means possible attained. Motives are not examined very critically, nor methods scanned too closely, because it is somehow complacently assumed that the means will find their complete justification in the end. Thus, alas! doth it come to pass that the worship of this strange god perverts the judgment, and blinds the eyes of the miserable devotees.

Oh! when will men try to keep in memory the most notable object lesson ever given to the world, the greatest defeat, or seeming defeat, resulting in the grandest victory—the Christ upon the cross. He did not seek victory. He simply and solely sought to do the will of His Father, and victory came without seeking. So will it come to every true servant of God, who, with pure intent, seeks to do and suffer His will, and is content to leave the results with Him, who is the only infallible judge of the times and seasons for the manifestation of His power in the outpouring of His Spirit upon men.

If the reader should conclude from these criticisms that I am opposed to revivals, let me inform him that he has come to a false conclusion, and one that the criticisms do not justify. I am not opposed to revivals. No true Christ's man can be, for it is thus, when God willeth, that the Divine Sovereignty, and the Almightiness of the Spirit are made conspicuously manifest for His own glory, and for the good of men; and even the world is compelled to look on with surprising wonder, and exclaim surely this is the power of God. When God works there is no mistake about it, and criticism is silenced because it is unnecessary, and, indeed, impossible.

What I object to is that human devices, however skilfully and successfully executed, should pass for Divine working. I know that God works through the human — that is, through the human presentation of a Divine message, but when the human is painfully conspicuous, far more conspicuous than the Divine, I have reason, and good reason, to be skeptical about the genuineness of the operations themselves, and of the results achieved; and I am compelled to accept at a considerable discount their possible ethical value.

And then again, it is a matter open to very serious speculation whether, after all, the ordinary level of Christian life is not perceptibly lowered by a constant and almost exclusive insistence upon one truth, however important, and the straining after large and immediate results upon the basis of that truth.

But you say, the truth is important and fundamental. I admit that it is, and for that very reason I insist that it shall be used as such. Lay it as a foundation, and the true foundation, and then go on and develop the other important truths, the understanding and assimilation of which, by the individual soul, are necessary to "growing unto a holy temple in the Lord."

A good foundation is of great and indispensable value in regard to the edifice that it is proposed to rear upon it, but apart from that it has no meaning, and is neither valuable nor useful. Indeed, it is worse than useless, for it is cumbering ground that might be more profitably occupied; and is unsightly and repugnant. And if we follow the analogy that comes to the surface here—and it is not unworthy of recognition—we shall plainly see why so many professing Christians are so useless and so unlovely in their lives; people who instead of being attractive are positively unattractive and repellant.

They professed faith in Christ, perhaps during some season of special interest, when excitement ran very high, and, may be, intelligent conviction ran correspondingly low. When the season was over they settled down into a conviction of security for time and for eternity, but they forgot all about the building operations that ought to have immediately followed. We look, expecting to see a manifest change in the life, and a fair super-structure of Christian character arise, as stone on stone is laid of pure and noble thoughts and deeds. But alas! we look in vain, in a great many instances. If there is not absolute vacancy, we see or hear only a confused mass of Pharisaical notions and ideas, interspersed, it may be, with vain exhortations to other people to believe, that would scarcely do credit to a parrot; a lot of " wood, hay, and stubble," which the first unfriendly wind or fire will scatter, or burn up.

But you say you are on the true foundation, and you know it. Then, in God's name, and for your own sake and others, set to work and build. Don't talk ; build. If you are satisfied the foundation is all right, and you say you are, let that conviction suffice for all time, and go straight on and build. Build something that God will sanction, that your own purest convictions will approve, and that men and angels may regard with favor, and give glory to God for it.

Go into the quarry of intelligent, unreserved obedience, and you will get there any amount of building material. No lack will you find, but enough and to spare. Eternity—to say nothing of time—will not exhaust it, for improvement and increase come by use. And as each stone is quarried, and cut, and polished, and put in its place under the eye of the Master, the fair super-structure of a consecrated manhood will arise, imposing and symmetrical, and like unto His because in obedience to Him. Obedience! Obedience to Christ! Yes, that makes a Christian what he should be, like unto his Lord. Not merely obedience to a few sacramental directions, but that of the whole life, heart, and soul. That builds character, guides conduct, and makes life pure and brave.

"Men of the 97th follow me," said the saintly Hedley Vicars as he leaped the trenches before Sebastapol, when his keen eye caught sight of the foe stealthily advancing under cover of darkness. "Follow me," he said again as he turned his face to beckon on his men, and with sword uplifted pointed out the way. Just at that moment a pale moonbeam smote the glittering blade, and illumined the face of that brave and saintly man, and at that moment he fell. The loved leader had led his last charge, and men with strong arms and beating hearts surrounded the prostrate form, and bore him back to his tent, where, in a few short hours, he breathed out his brave, sweet life.

Thus died Captain Hedley Vicars. A man of rare qualities of mind and heart. His Christianity was as conspicuous as his regimentals. He served Christ as faithfully and as bravely as he served his Queen and country. He was a lovable man; loved by all who knew him, and deeply lamented in death, especially by the men of the 97th who knew he was brave, and knew he was a Christian.

Perchance he learned that battle cry from the captain he so fervently loved, and so faithfully served. " Follow me" fell from the lips of the greatest leader of men the world has ever known, or ever will. It has come down the centuries to us not with diminished but with added force by the lapse of time ; and when it is fully understood and heeded, by all who believe in Him, there will be such an awakening, and such a manifestation of spiritual life and power, as this round globe has never yet witnessed.

Far off as this brighter dawn may seem, it is coming, surely coming. Coming, not with blare of trumpet and loud acclaim, but as the light cometh, silently, softly, yet irresistibly. Coming, in the pure radiance of consecrated lives, reflecting "the brightness of His glory, and the express image of His person." In that day, that which was proclaimed from the beginning, as the proof and bond of Christian brotherhood, will be universally accepted: "Whosoever shall do the will of My Father which is in heaven, the same is my brother, and sister, and mother."

THE END.

www.ingramcontent.com/pod-product-compliance
Lightning Source LLC
Chambersburg PA
CBHW032052220426
43664CB00008B/973